Dilemmas of Being in Business

by

Dr. Rosie Kuhn

Copyright

What People are Saying about *Dilemmas of Being in Business*

"Dr. Kuhn's latest book, *The Dilemmas of Being in Business,* hits a bull's-eye into the heart of the matter. Where many people engage in the conversation about job satisfaction by learning new business skills or enhancing one's ability to navigate corporate politics, Dr. Kuhn strikes the mark exactly where it resides: The discontent lives within the domain of our humanity. It is there that dilemmas manifest, and ultimately it is there where it is resolved, most readily with the support of a skilled coach/thinking partner. Everything else is just dancing around the issue. Dr. Kuhn's skillful description of the circumstances within which her clients find themselves and the way she helps them peel back layers to reveal the core issue and ultimately define their solution, all while guiding the reader to the kernel of truth within *their* own lives, reveals many "ah has." Quick! Read this book, find a great coach and move your work life to the next level!" *Carmella Granado Senior Director of Organizational Effectiveness, Flextronics,*

"Bringing forth true Spirit at work is a challenge for leaders, in the US and globally. Dr. Rosie Kuhn shares the journey she's taking, coaching to inspire greater self-awareness and insights, with business and community leaders pursuing values-honoring lives. Her keen observations and candid feedback provide readers with substance, guidance, and the lessons learned by those walking their paths." *Gretchen M. Krampf, MSOD, PCC, Principal of Process Experts, LLC*

"At the juxtaposition of positive organizational behavior, positive psychology and transpersonal psychology, one finds Dr. Rosie Kuhn and her writing on survival and success in today's workplaces. In this book, Rosie describes through coaching case stories how she has helped her clients discover, explore and choose between options in the seemingly hopeless situations, but absolutely typical ones we all face. Don't look to this book for a quick fix, but do look to it as a wonderful guide to help understand: how and why one perceives their work environment; uncover the choices and decisions that need to be made in those environments; utilize this knowledge to act in alignment with what's best for the organization, its people and the individual." *Larry Bonham, CTO, SoulFriends.com*

"As a 13 year Senior Product Line Manager in the Service Provider Technology Group at Cisco Systems I'm faced with many daily obstacles and challenges. One of those challenges is dealing with people to whom I perceive myself smarter than – I believe, initially, that I always have the better solution. Only now, after reading Rosie's book, do I realize there are different approaches to dealing with complex situations. *Dilemmas of Being in Business* clarifies that there are no right answers, just different paths through the complex world of business." *Donyel A. Jones-Williams, Cisco Systems*

"Dr. Kuhn has created a fascinating opportunity to do something most have forgotten how to do – Think! She forces us to look closely at ourselves and think about who we are, what we want and how we'll get it. She also makes us more aware that we need to better understand how we choose to appear and interact with others. Her writing takes us down an avenue thick with commonsense, and the message is that we need to *take time to think things through.* This is a book one should reread at least once a month." *Leslie R. Wolff, CEO/Chief Marketing Strategist at the Smart Marketing Group, author, lecturer and apostle of "Outthinking your competition, rather than outspending them."*

"Real People, Real Situations and Real Dilemmas. That's what you will find in this tale of everyday people in the everyday business world. You'll read of Harry, and how most people overlook the real question that he and each of us must ask and answer. And you will read of Mei-Li, who was born in China, earned her Ph.D., moved to Silicon Valley and now struggles with balancing work and personal happiness. And, Harry and Mei-Li are just the beginning; Frank, Hank, Brandy, Nancy, Will, Michael, Madeleine, and others: Each of them has a similar story – a story around the everyday dilemmas that we all have, or will encounter over the course of our own personal career paths.... Highly recommended." *Bruce Boston, Sr. Data Scientist, Cupertino, CA*

"Employing powerful personal narratives and a keen sense of humor, Dr. Kuhn unravels common dilemmas in business and life in an emotionally and intellectually accessible way helping readers identify and approach these circumstances thoughtfully and with an openness to alternative ways of knowing and being." *Ellen Klein, Ethicist, Health-Communications, University of South Florida*

"Dr. Rosie Kuhn has both the experience and the multiple degrees to write one of those dense and unreadable books about the psychology of business and how to solve complicated business problems. Don't worry: this book is the complete opposite of that. It is practical, personal and powerful information you can apply in your business today. It tells interesting stories you can relate to as examples of how to solve *your* dilemmas in *your* business. It prescribes clear actions you can take today to move from problem to solution in your business. Whether you are from corporate, in a partnership, or are a solo-preneur, this is a book you should read and apply right now. By reading this 'real world' book, you will see new opportunities in your people, yourself and your business. Solving the dilemmas of being in business goes right to the bottom line. Buy it, read it, apply it, and be more successful, starting now. Thanks for making it simple Dr. Kuhn." *Hans Phillips Performance Consultant, Ontoco.com*

Dedication

Carmella Granado walks in two worlds, the human/spiritual world and the corporate world of Silicon Valley, CA. Anyone exposed to Carmella immediately experiences the utmost respect, honor and compassion. Within hours of working with her, they have fallen in love with themselves – yes, corporate leaders and executives! They become curious about who they are and how they impact the world. In the presence of Carmella, they expand their business intelligence to include their humanity and the humanity of those with whom they engage. They realize that working smarter, not harder, with softer hearts and bigger smiles transforms their workplace, making it a far more productive and satisfying environment to be in.

Transformation occurs on a daily basis in this particular corporation, which spans the globe with over 200,000 employees. They all feel the effects of one Carmella Granado.

I dedicate this book to you, Carmella. Thank you for all that you are and all that you bring.

Table of Contents

Introduction

My clients are extraordinary people. Each is invested in expanding their breadth of wisdom, in service to bringing the fullest expression of essential self to their profession and life in general. Each is engaged in high-stakes ventures and understands that in order to fulfill their mission, they have to think outside their current paradigm. They've chosen to hire a thinking partner (me) who will support and empower them to generate the outcome of their vision. This is only possible by cultivating intelligence, a practice that supports, among other things, the removal of bankrupt interpretations about who they are and what they are doing in the world of business.

Most of us believe that the inherent gifts and talents found in extraordinary people are what make them extraordinary. It is so much more than that! Extraordinary people accept that they have been gifted, and in gratitude for these gifts, they cultivate and nourish the environment within themselves so that their gifts and talents can expand into the fullest expression of their essential nature.

Fulfilling a company's vision isn't based on action alone. It is based on actions that come from cultivated awareness. Extraordinary people willingly challenge limiting beliefs that interfere with the fullest utilization of their gifts and talents. They know there is effortless access to a wisdom far beyond their comprehension. They know it is readily available only by getting out of their own way.

Throughout these pages, you'll be reading about extraordinary people meeting ordinary experiences, being stymied and stumped just like us ordinary folk. The difference between them and us is that they willingly penetrate and explore the edge of reason of their current paradigm. They face personal demons in dilemmas that surface throughout everyday life and, they choose to see things differently so their intentions may be realized. It isn't that they are fearless and courageous beyond measure; it's that they are curious to know what lies beyond the signpost that reads: "DANGER: DO NOT ENTER." They want to expand their repertoire and capacity to choose differently when facing unknown territory. They comprehend that there is a wisdom beyond their own level of expertise that will guide and assist them into more expansive and effective leadership. They are scared, just like the rest of us; however they act regardless of the fear.

The dilemmas that I address in this book are universal and relevant to transforming the corporate environment. All identifying factors have been changed to protect the privacy of my clients, their companies and organizations.

I am inspired to write what I do because of the issues that arise for every one of my corporate clients. I continue to be inspired by their dilemmas because they are telling of the challenges they face for themselves and the organizations they work with. It's the choice-points that each of us grapples with and which turn ordinary people into extraordinary.

The intention of this book is to introduce a way of thinking that empowers choice-makers like you to see more clearly how you choose to choose what you choose in regard to the work you do, the people you work with and yourself. While in your work environment, there is never a time when you are not making choices in relation to these three aspects. You are always juggling, prioritizing and reprioritizing in order to feel a sense of balance, fulfillment and control.

How you choose to balance and prioritize anything is based on your hierarchy of commitments. Your top commitment is usually what you say out loud. At the same time, additional commitments call for attention, which creates, more often than not, internal conflicts of interest. What this can feel like is that we are stuck, confused, anxious and stressed. Progress happens too slowly and the cause has yet to be determined.

When we are able to distinguish the many aspects of life and work to which we are committed, we are then able to make sense of the competing factors that pull us in opposing directions. This puts us in a dilemma. Normally, we don't know what to choose or how to choose to choose. So, we sit in this dilemma, at the choice-point, waiting and hoping for something to steer us in the right direction. Regardless of your position on the corporate ladder, in this moment, you are most likely sitting at a choice-point – waiting and hoping.

Dilemmas of Being in Business explores a number of aspects of corporate and business life. Each allows us to dive into a deeper investigation, revealing conflicting commitments. With curiosity, we explore various styles of being and doing that can help us navigate any number of choice-points, in service to the highest truth and good of your organization and all of those associated with you.

I'll share with you my model, from which I clearly distinguish the reality or circumstance as it appears (Domain of Circumstance); the way we choose to act, think and be, regarding our circumstance (Domain of Self-Empowerment); the aspect of our being that has us either feel inadequate, unworthy and unlovable, and continually on alert that we will be found out; and the aspect of our being that knows without question that we are brilliant, creative, lovable and visionary – and which continually pushes for our fullest expression of self (Domain of Humanity).

Domain of
UNIVERSAL ONENESS

Domain of
HUMANITY

Domain of
SELF-EMPOWERMENT

Domain of
CIRCUMSTANCES

DOMAINS OF AWARENESS

You can see that I also include the Domain of Universal Source/Oneness, from which we've all come, and with which we continually relate. Also known as our higher power, God, Goddess, etc, it is to this we pray, talk, or, for some, ignore and deny any relationship at all. It's the unknowable, the mystery that is everywhere and is

14

always impacting our human experience. As I said, we generally ignore its presence and influence in our lives until we feel powerless, helpless and hopeless. Understanding that we are not our circumstances, nor our choices, nor even our humanity, gives us an opportunity to be with the questions – "If I'm not that, then what am I? And, if I'm more than what I appear to be, how do I access, utilize and optimize this higher wisdom and intelligence?"

It's not as though this conversation isn't going on inside you without your knowledge or consent. It actually never stops! It's just that your hierarchy of commitments may obscure the ongoing conversation you have with this higher wisdom; to the degree that it's barely a whisper among the din of circumstances, survival needs and pleasures sought.

I am a life and business coach. What I'm sharing with you here is much of what I share with all my corporate clients. I empower them to empower themselves to acknowledge the current dilemma that has them have to choose between what they say they want, and conflicting commitments which they want, but not as much as their spoken commitment.

How to choose to choose what they choose while at this choice-point is no different from how many of you choose to choose what you choose. Throughout this book, you'll have fun, hopefully, being curious about how other people 'be with' their dilemmas, and you'll also explore and experiment with the dilemmas of being you in business.

1: What is it Like When You are Smarter than Your Boss

You and a colleague, Harry, are up for a promotion. You know you are the better person for the job, but Harry gets the position. He's pompous, arrogant and doesn't have the leadership skills that inspire you to generate, well, anything. You scratch your head in disbelief that he was chosen over you. And, you begin to strategize how you will endure working under Harry.

For some reason, even though the whole office knows of Harry's incompetence, no one takes action. He's that one rotten apple that spoils the whole barrel. You may want to sabotage Harry's efforts and do whatever you can to expose him for the inadequate, incompetent individual that you see him to be. However, that goes against your integrity and you may end up looking bad and feeling worse in the end.

There are a lot of Harry's and Harriet's in the business world. Whatever your position at your firm, you know you are smarter than your boss. You deserve his/her salary and every perk that goes along with it, because you are working your butt off while s/he's the one looking good! AAARRRGGHH!

If you go above Harry's head to his boss, Glenda, you might not only aggravate Harry but also reveal to

Glenda that she may have made a choice that's now creating negative consequences far beyond any expectations. She's already regretting her choice and knows there's nothing she can do. Having you approach her with your complaints will make her feel worse about her decision.

This scenario is not uncommon. Probably 30% of my business clients are struggling with at least one particular individual that is a thorn in their side. They question their own sanity and the sanity of those who put the Harry's of the world in these positions. What do you do? It's a dilemma.

Do you stay or do you go? Do you ask for a transfer? Do you stay and suck it up, because you need the job? Do you try to go around Harry, or do you do what you do best and ignore what Harry wants from you?

My job as a transformational coach is not to fix, heal or convert clients, so they'll have the answers to problems that they face. My job is to be a thinking partner, empowering clients to unravel all of the complexities that bring him or her to this dilemma and choice-point.

Our business systems are no different from our family systems, in that they are generated and driven by survival mechanisms that most likely operate from a fear-based paradigm. They have been cultivated through generations of personal relationships, based on familial, cultural, religious, and gender factors. Too often wisdom and common sense do not enter into the equation when it comes to how a business or family operates. We take for granted and assume intelligence and maturity would be foundational to choosing directors, managers and leaders, but trust me, and you may know from your own experience, most people running businesses, departments and corporations function, to some degree, from the emotional intelligence of an adolescent. It makes sense that you are going to think you are smarter than your boss. In some ways you probably are; in other ways you probably aren't.

The trick is to notice this pattern of operating. When you're feeling smarter than – what's the quality of this experience? Are you feeling righteous and arrogant, contemptuous and condescending? Do you feel frustrated and discouraged? What actions are you likely to take from righteous, condescending, frustrated and discouraged? What do you do to compensate for feeling this way? How do you avoid, distract, ignore or deny your own part in this dysfunctional process? By the way, we are all participating in having the Harry's of the world be where they are. You are no exception!

The questions funnel down to just one: *What is it you are here to learn that puts Harry in your life, in this time, in this way?* Answer this question and you'll understand what it is you need to shift in order to facilitate the learning. I guarantee that while doing what's required in order to make the shift, you'll notice that Harry will either change or go away! It's fascinating to observe what changes within our environment, once we 'get' our part in maintaining the status quo.

Entangled and embroiled in the cauldron of complexity of your work environment, it can be challenging to see all of this without a thinking partner or coach who can hold the bigger picture, and who also holds you accountable for your participation in the unfolding of your life within this bigger picture. No coach or thinking partner? That's okay. Just be willing to be truthful in answering the questions above. This alone will create a positive shift for you, and the Harry's of the world will go POOF!

By the way, some of the Harry's of the world are my clients too. Given an opportunity to look at what has them choose to choose 'how they be,' they, too, willingly shift in support of a larger, more fulfilling outcome. Yay for us all!

2: Angry SOB's are Lovable Too

One of my clients, Bart, is actually a Harry kind of guy. Bart makes people wrong whenever they disagree with him. He makes his clients feel like imbeciles when their suggestions are different from his. He has to be right about everything, regardless of the fact that it is oppressive and demeaning for those who work for him.

Bart rules based on control and domination. He uses his power to disempower others so he can feel more in control. He always looks for reasons to make others wrong so he can feel righteous. By feeling righteous he feels invulnerable to attack.

At the same time, Bart's use of power doesn't allow him to really connect with his employees; this contributes to dissatisfaction in all parts of his life. He envies his General Manager, Marc, because Marc has a great relationship with the employees. They are happy and work effectively for Marc, because he leads with his heart and they like that. Bart doesn't know how to do this yet.

When all is said and done, Bart realizes that what he wants to gain from our coaching relationship is more fulfillment in his personal and professional life. He is beginning to understand that to experience a greater degree of fulfillment means he must allow himself to dismantle his current interpretation or context around power and his use of it.

To empower himself to have more fulfillment, consistently, at this point, Bart is willing to practice being powerful in a different way. He is unsure about what he'll find, and who he is without invulnerability-oriented practices of power. He doesn't yet realize that it means shifting perceptions and practices wherever he goes.

Bart's dilemma is that he only knows one way to feel listened to and respected. As a young boy, his mom and dad disregarded his thoughts and feelings. His needs and wants were ignored; his parents couldn't see or appreciate the human child that so desperately required attention in order to feel valued and important. Nearly forty years of age, Bart is practicing a survival strategy that worked when no one would listen to him: he got angry and controlling. Though this strategy works to achieve a feeling of control and importance, it doesn't work to experience the fulfillment that comes with authentic connection and working relationships. This would require him to dismantle the thinking system that supports the current strategy he has in place.

Angry, controlling individuals act the way they do because it makes them feel invulnerable. Inside these "SOB's" are innocent, vulnerable children – just like the rest of us, who don't quite know how to be loved or loving, and aren't even sure they want to know – it's too scary!

Bart faces this inevitable dilemma: Do I stay invulnerable, controlling and gruff, which minimizes my fulfillment in life? Or do I learn to be vulnerable, which allows for greater fulfillment and an expansion of my capacity to empower others without disempowering myself, personally and professionally?

Depending on how entrenched a person is in their belief systems, and the strategies that support those beliefs, this could be a long and painful process, or it could shift quickly. We never know until we begin to step into the expedition. Bart is pretty entrenched and isn't yet aware of all the ramifications that come with postponing the inevitable demise of his old paradigm.

When we don't pay attention to the subtle cues that change is required, more likely than not we'll feel a powerful nudge, a push, then a shove. If we still haven't gotten the message we'll experience an AAAAHHHHHH! moment – very different from an Ah-Ha moment. The AAAAHHHHHHHH! moment is when we say, "Where the hell did that come from; I never saw it coming!" By this time, we hurt like hell, feel helpless and have no idea where to turn for help or support. Too often, we've lost family and friends, jobs, security – well, everything! I'm not making this stuff up! And, those of you who've gone through this process know what I'm talking about.

We are given plenty of opportunities to discover what we came here to learn with little pain or effort. Because we have been trained to acquiesce to the 'shoulds' and 'shouldn'ts' within our Domain of Circumstance, we lose our ability to be intelligent. We begin to make assumptions about reality that just don't make sense. Bart believes he can be respected and important by bullying his employees. Raise your hand if you agree this is intelligent choice-making.

Similar to Bart, all of us operate under specific beliefs and truths about power and relationship, which make no sense to others. The dilemma each of us face is whether we are willing to cultivate and exercise intelligence in service to what we desire, while letting go of a style of being and doing that makes us feel invulnerable. Only through exploring and experimenting will each of us – including Bart, find our way.

3: Good Choice – Disappointing Outcome

My client Madeleine was recently hired as the financial manager for an international corporation. She is currently overwhelmed because she is learning the ropes of her new position. Meanwhile, she's also in the midst of hiring new staff. She's in a pickle.

Carl, a direct report of Madeleine's, who used to be a co-worker before Madeleine's promotion, is, and has been unhappy for a long time. Carl has complained to Madeleine for years, and now that Madeleine is in a position to do something to help Carl, there's nothing she can, because she's understaffed and overwhelmed. Carl is threatening to leave, which would put Madeleine into deeper angst. She can't afford to lose Carl and at the same time, she can't afford the time and energy consumed by his needs. This is a dilemma for Madeleine.

Madeleine is committed to fulfilling her duties, defined by her boss, who oversees the European Market. She needs Carl to stay and do what's required in order to fulfill his commitment. She is also committed to ensuring her colleagues and direct reports that they are being served effectively by her leadership. She knows that it would be best to let Carl leave, but how will she manage?

Being in such a dilemma challenges managers and executives alike. Is there a win-win situation here, or is Madeleine facing a win-lose, or, your basic no one wins this time around? Sometimes that happens, you know.

One aspect of my work as a thinking partner that I enjoy is sitting with my clients in dilemmas such as Madeleine's. Together we explore what's possible. Given that within this current circumstance any outcome will create some degree of frustration for Madeleine, she still has to choose which outcome will create the least amount of stress on her, her team and the company. It takes a lot of presence and maturity to be with such a dilemma.

How does one handle such a circumstance? It's a big fat 'be-with;' a circumstance that challenges Madeleine's sense of responsibility, reliability and integrity as a company officer. She's struggling with her identity as a person who manages, and as an individual her team can count on.

It's not that she can't do the work; it's not that she's ineffective; in this moment her circumstances provide challenges in which she thinks she needs to get it all done, and done perfectly; however this is impossible, given her current situation.

There's No Right or Wrong, Good or Bad, in a Situation Like This

The Domain of Self-Empowerment is where we make choices based on what we want as our desired outcome, while minimizing the possibility of our undesired outcome. Within Madeleine's Domain of Self-Empowerment, she's looking for perfect. The Domain of Humanity, the human aspect in each of us, fears for our job, reputation, respect and trust. We cough out strategies, attempting to put out fires as quickly as possible so no one will find out or decide that we are incompetent and replaceable – something we all fear.

As long as we are afraid someone will find out or decide that we are not enough, like Madeleine, we will forever attempt to cover our tracks. We leave no room for errors; and, oh, by the way, we rarely bring our best to the game, nor will we innovate and create to our fullest expression. There's too much at stake.

Exhausted and overwhelmed, Madeleine is prioritizing her commitments, and then organizing her thinking to reflect those commitments. Something or someone may have to be sacrificed. How does she choose? Does she choose to choose based on her fear that her boss will reprimand her for her lack of performance? Does she choose to choose based on already being overwhelmed, and that losing Carl will put her under even further? Is there another way to look at her scenario? Is there another place from which to choose?

We all face moments like these, in our work and personal life, when there is a no-win situation. I don't think it matters that Madeleine is new to this level of management and leadership; she's up to her eyeballs in alligators. Now what?

Here is my point. We can't get it right all the time. When we can't get it right, how do we 'be with' the current dilemma, especially when there appears to be so much at stake?

Corporations run as if every second counts. Madeleine's dilemma will stop the clock one way or another. So assessing, not from panic, fear, nor inadequacies, but from what choice will be most effective, is the key. Choosing to choose from grounded clarity, while willingly relinquishing the fear of the consequences – that is what good managers and leaders do. You make your best-calculated guess, and then let go. If you've done your best – what more could you expect of yourself? As the saying goes, you gotta let the chips fall where they may.

This is the most challenging place to be for any corporate or businessperson. We have to let go of our attachment to doing it right in order to please everyone. Choosing from integrity and professional wisdom is the best any of us can do. Why barrage ourselves with self-deprecation, self-doubt and criticism? Allow the chips to fall and focus on the you that has done the best. Acknowledge the challenge and be with the experience that comes with failing to be perfect, liked and appreciated.

The most effective leaders and managers in any business setting choose without fear of the consequences. It takes courage to take a stand for your competence, your choice-making and who you are behind the role at work.

Madeleine is actually in a perfect situation. She is facing certain failure, as she will face many times in her career. This is an opportunity for her to explore the territory of the 'Big-Fat-Be-With.' In doing so, she will realize a deeper, stronger, more resourceful Self; one that will no longer be controlled by fear. She will look back to this experience to remember the process of being with certain failure while succeeding at bringing her very best to the situation.

4: *Growing Pains*

A client of mine, Nancy, called me yesterday somewhat distressed. She is in product management at an international corporation, headquartered in Silicon Valley, CA.

A few months ago, Nancy read a book by Robin Sharma – *The Leader Who Had No Title*. She began practicing some of the exercises, which allowed her to stretch and expand her comfort zone to include more of her authentic leadership style. The dilemma though, is that as she exercises and stretches to expand her repertoire, she's experiencing growing pains that bring with them discomfort, uncertainty, fear and insecurity. She is finding it distressful and uncomfortable to shift the way she shows up in her work. She's uncertain if it will make her more attractive for promotions and all that goes along with them. She knows she's on the right track with regard to cultivating greater professionalism and effectiveness, yet she has doubts whether these traits truly make a difference in the corporate world, where flash and charm often win the promotion. Will she gain more visibility and be acknowledged for what she brings to the role of leader? She's in a dilemma.

As we change and grow, we discard what no longer serves, and often find ourselves in the midst of a leap of faith. It's very exciting yet disconcerting at the same time. With practice, the long-term reward is a growing ability to evolve into the person and leader we say we want to be.

There are those who expect that with the right education and connections it will be easy to rise to the top. There are those who play the game the right way and anticipate that the right way will get them the outcome they want. No one really knows for sure, and too often, we lose our souls along the way.

As Nancy lets go of her suitable education, her connections and playing the game appropriately, in service to exploring authentic leadership styles, she is triggered and collapses into feeling anxious, weak, vulnerable and unworthy. She shares that, in some moments, she loses her balance and can hardly stand up.

Nancy is a model of resiliency. There are many who cannot stand being triggered into feeling vulnerable, weak and inadequate, and they do whatever they can to avoid this experience. Their unwillingness to cultivate and strengthen this essential capacity will inevitably bring about consequences worse than the loss of a promotion. Nancy is taking personal and professional risks that on the inside feel, sometimes, as though she is failing and will never recover. It's a debilitating momentary feeling, yet she knows that to do it any other way is out of integrity – a consequence worse than the loss of a promotion.

This intense practice develops muscles required for the type of leaders most organizations are truly hungry for. What's at stake for Nancy is her personal identity as a winner and as a perfectionist. She's putting it all on the line because she knows her current choice-making fails to serve her organization in the way she aspires to – as a leader who puts aside personal needs and desires for the sake of the people she works with and for.

Even though there are tons of books on the market about leadership development, so few people actually take up the practice of shifting their personal perspective to something greater, from personal gain to professional integrity. Cultivating self-awareness while developing leadership capacities can be an angst-filled experience. Yet the reward is mastery, and the elimination of manipulations and political motivations inconsistent with corporate visions and statements of integrity.

I suggest to Nancy that she see herself to be the experiment – an exploration. What makes her valuable to her company, in my mind, is that she is willing to be in the "I don't know," discovering what's beyond the games, political motivations and manipulations that actually limit possibilities within most organizations.

Through this process Nancy is learning that she isn't supposed to know or to have the easier or 'right' way to move through such a transformation. She is only to observe, witness, notice and assess what works and what doesn't. Then, shift how she is being and what she is doing. Then, again notice, witness, observe and assess. This is the path to mastery, innovation, inspiration, freedom and selfless leadership.

As any one of us, like Nancy, cultivates the resilience to move through this process, we'll be developing not only wisdom and mastery but we'll be able to empower others to explore, witness, and experiment as well. This to me is the most powerful form of leadership – making space for others to explore, experiment and discover their own innovative styles of leading.

The dilemma – that choice-point between one type of success and the other, each pulling Nancy and keeping her on the fence, happens far less so than before. What she is currently practicing – where she is putting her attention, will inevitably bring her into the light, because she acknowledges and honors her highest truth. My belief is that this is the sustainable, healthier and more effective way to lead. It will be recognized for its value – growing pains and all.

This is not an easy path, nor should it be. To truly be a great leader, rather than follow the well-worn path, we need to become the experiment, embracing the moments when our findings are thrilling and monumental in their effects.

5: Ignoring What We Know to Be True

I deny aspects of me that I know to be true – those dark shadowy characteristics that, if people were to find out – well, it could mean rejection, humiliation and annihilation. It's best that I pretend they don't exist. DENIAL: Don't Even Know I Am Lying!

On the other hand I have a knowing of certain truths, yet I deny myself this wisdom as well. I use doubt and uncertainty as strategies, which diminish my potential and visibility in the world. In past lives, I've probably been murdered or tortured for standing out beyond the norm. "Won't do that again," I say to myself. Yet, living within the protective cocoon of my denial, fear and pretending is also torturous.

Many of my executive clients over the years have experienced a 360-degree evaluation process, whereby they ask for feedback from people they work and live with. An enormous amount of information is generated, assessed and returned to these individuals so they can see how others perceive them, and what they can shift in order to be more effective in their roles.

These 360 processes are valuable, and yet, my clients share that most of what is said isn't new to them. They are already aware of what they do well and what they need to enhance, grow and develop. They already know!

I always find this fascinating that we know what we know, yet live and work as if we don't. We wait to have our internal wisdom, knowledge and experience validated by the external world. WHY?

When people do bad things and are brought to justice, they say, "I knew it was wrong and punishable, but spare me, please."

This is crazy-making. We have the wisdom to know right from wrong, and a knowing beyond what makes sense in our cause-and-effect world. Yet we choose to deny our culpability and our God-given powers to be the fullest expression of the gifts of our being.

I finished a book last week by Michael Sky, called *Jubilee Day – A Novel*. It is about our current circumstances regarding those who hold power in the United States, how they use that power, and the opportunity to choose differently. It's a brilliant book!

Most of us use our power for egoic gains. We don't stop ourselves. We also use our power to distract ourselves from the internal knowing that, if nothing else, we are violating our own integrity and the dignity of our soul. We know, and we pretend we don't know.

For those of us who attend church every Saturday and Sunday, hearing over and over the importance of using our power in support of all people, too often we ignore opportunities to practice what we preach when we enter our Monday through Friday Church of the business environment. We are faced with a dilemma: Do I do what I know to be in the highest good of all – my company, employees, my own soul, or do I act from my personal desire for gain, safety, security and control? There is so much at stake!

Each individual teeters on the brink of personal annihilation. The devastation we witness in all aspects of our Global system is only a reflection of what's occurring within each of us. When the current and flow of a Universal and natural unfolding is ignored, diverted or stopped, in service to our insatiable hunger for power and invulnerability, we inevitably come face-to-face with the consequences of our choice-making. Funny how it works that way!

If you've ever been around adolescents, you've noticed they often have an attitude of absolute invulnerability. They are super powers unto themselves. As parents of adolescents, hopefully we remember our own teenage years when we felt we knew everything and no one could tell us any differently. As adults, we know it's a stage in the learning process and that there will be a day of reckoning when these teenagers fall off their pedestal and realize they are human, just like the rest of us.

I think about the European Countries who have been around far longer than the US. In their youth they built empires and were super powers. All have been demolished, or have fallen into ruin, only to be rebuilt from a more mature perspective. I see the more dignified and wise countries smiling at the U.S., knowing of our youthful "no one will take us down" attitude. It is part of the process of maturing – of losing what we've not rightfully gained, in order to cultivate a more mature relationship with our currency of resources – the earth, our people, our Selves – all of it.

The dilemma we face as individuals is that we are committed to holding onto our super power ideation, yet, at the same time we are conscious of the cost of ignoring the fact that we can no longer build skyscrapers in the air. We hope we'll get away with it, but ...

Pretending that choosing to choose not to choose will keep us invulnerable to our human frailties is adolescent thinking at best. Inevitably, our commitment to avoiding mature and wise choice-making will lead us to a phenomenal human experience called despair. Despair is when we realize that the reality of our own creation – our skyscrapers in the air, are coming down, detonated by our own ignoring – not ignorance.

All of us face dilemmas that inevitably put us in the line of fire of our own humanity. It's your call to make life-choices consciously or unconsciously. From my point of view, it's far more fun to powerfully engage in life, fully awake, conscious and mature. You already know what I'm talking about.

GWLN This week I'm attending a leadership conference sponsored by the Global Women's Leadership Network (GWLN), based in Santa Clara, California. Eighteen women from all over the world come together to develop leadership skills in order to bring change to their villages, communities, countries and the world.

These eighteen women show up unarmed yet prepared to do battle, understanding the gifts of their enemies. I've rarely seen such passion, compassion, love and inspired wisdom with which they take on issues of health, water, nutrition, literacy, equality and empowerment for all. They know that violence does not feed nor clothe the people most in need. They see the phenomenal human resource in individuals, who, to most of us, are just starving, sick and illiterate.

They are prepared to combat aspects of the world and their own personal belief system that strive to put a stop to what seems like an impossible mission. In one short week, these women become an unstoppable force and part of a growing number who see a future that is worth fighting for. There is no talk of violence or discrimination; no consideration of how to kill the enemy, for they know that only by receiving the gifts from their enemies will they transform the world.

While these women face many dilemmas they see possibility. They are a "Yes, We Can!" group of people. They know that ultimately their visions will be fulfilled, because they say so. They've witnessed more than one hundred women and two men, who have gone through the GWLN program, fulfill on their promises to bring water, medical centers, libraries and more to the people they support and empower.

Living into a passionate call to serve is inspiring, yet challenges abound. Politics – such as running for office is one thing, but one faces rejection as well. Additionally, organizations that support grass roots efforts have a lot of power to give and take away funds. How does an individual create or be an invitation that will give them access to funding?

Throughout the world, some who are committed enough to change the environment for women and children know that entering politics is a very risky business. The possibility of violence against these women, their families and others is a real threat.

These women are the CEOs of the future. Most likely they will never do a round of 360s for their organization. Their hearts and vision steer them in the direction of fulfilling their best contribution to the world with accountability to the people they serve. They understand the life and death matters of their leadership.

6: Gift Me with My Enemies and My Ministers

I woke from a dream this morning that made me question: "Really?" It was only the last few seconds of the dream that seemed so profound. A boys' choir was singing a Christmas song. The only lyric I heard was: "Gift me with my enemies and my ministers." This is a pretty profound phrase, especially for a group of youngsters to be singing as a Christmas song. It certainly gave me something to think about.

My enemies infuse me with intense emotions – rage, hatred, vile condemnation and contempt. Judgments are automatic, so much so I don't even know that I'm judging. How I respond, more often than not, is a knee jerk reaction. I'm inflamed and my actions are inflammatory. I want to violate them as they have violated me and my sense of what's right and wrong, good and bad. I want to wipe them off the planet so I can live peacefully. However …

What I know is that my enemies are my best teachers. They reflect what I most hate in the world and, most likely (like about 100% of the time), they reflect aspects of myself that I do not wish to acknowledge or own. When my enemies are around, I have no doubt, I have something to learn.

Ministers are also my teachers, my coaches and counselors. They are my thinking partners, who, through deep listening and questioning, reflect back to me how aligned I am with my highest truths. They also show me how I may be ignoring or distracting myself from the ways I've contributed to the very violence I hate in my adversaries. These wise beings bring my attention to the learnings so available to me by embracing my enemy as a long-lost lover.

Sometimes, though, in the company of my enemies, I retreat, hide and disappear into a myriad of disguises to protect myself from harm and looking bad. I may throw stones from behind a barrier and pretend it's not me at all who is engaged in warfare. I disown my anger, righteousness and indignation. "It wasn't me!" I exclaim with defensiveness and contempt for having been accused unjustly.

My ministers inquire into my actions, curious as to the origins of my behavior and the thoughts that precipitated them. What has me be blinded to my own truth – in denial (Don't Even Know I am Lying) of my barbarous attitude and position?

We need our enemies to confront us. They bring out the worst in us and provide opportunities for us to truly reflect on the importance, value and priorities of our hierarchy of desires. We need our ministers, counselors, therapists and coaches to reflect what gifts are available to us by engaging with our enemies.

The Dilemma

Many of us love to hate! It makes us feel good to think violent thoughts and even go to war for what we believe to be right and true. I often fantasize how I can get even or better yet, how I can be victorious over them. And then I think: What if I consider the possibility that my enemies are gifts? What would that mean – what consequences would unfold from such a consideration?

I'll tell you right now, I hate the thought of giving up my armor of righteousness and entitlement. Why? Because when I can wield my weapons with stealth and accuracy, I feel safe, powerful and in control. I love that feeling! And, without them, I believe myself to be defenseless, exposed and vulnerable.

I ask myself – what's considered right? What's considered wrong? Who is responsible for the woes of the world? My ministers smile and with their eyes inquire into my soul's wisdom for what is true. For that moment only, I comprehend that I am an accomplice in all acts of violence on the planet. Only by recognizing the seed of vengeance within me am I able to receive the gifts of freedom from my enemy.

Through deep discernment and the support and empowering nature of my ministers I am able to choose to choose to see my enemies and myself differently. Through the annihilation of my own pretence and the shattering of the barriers between us, I am truly allowed to realize I am my brother/sister's keeper, and they are mine.

The dilemma as a choice-point shifts when and how I choose to honor my highest truth and risk losing my attachments, my position, my identity – perhaps even life itself, for something much larger than me. I'm working on it!

7: Success – Where Does it Lead

Harvey, a client of mine for over four years, lives and works in LA in the television industry. Brilliant, creative and kind, he makes everyone feel appreciated by his character and presence. Harvey has finally arrived at his dream. Not only does he have the dream job for himself, he's also getting paid what he's worth. He is in the groove!

Harvey grew up in the bible belt of Texas. So, allowing himself to be worthy of a salary that reflects all of what he brings to his career was a huge undertaking. It went against the primary tenets of his childhood religion: that money is evil, and we shouldn't want material comforts. The underlying conflict between being spiritual and making enough money to thrive has been an underpinning of Harvey's financial demise for most of his adult life. Now, in his mid-forties, he's taken the steps required to receive the full benefits and reap the rewards of all he brings to his work life. Success!

This happened all within the past two months. So, Harvey has been adjusting to a whole new reality – money, prestige, a new BMW motorcycle and more. And …

What I love about Harvey is that he is very much awake. He sees that arriving at his desired destination doesn't mean the journey is over. He knows that in many ways, a new journey has just begun.

I was unsure what would show up in our coaching conversation once Harvey had fully owned his worth, asked for a raise, got it and so much more. What did arise had me breathe a sigh of relief. Harvey realized that the money, the position and the motorcycle does not bring an individual to a sense of fulfillment but for just a few brief ecstatic moments.

To see the striving for more money, prestige and power as just that, takes a dismantling of what we believe to be the only reality. To see the striving as a spiritual practice changes the attachment to the outcome, to something that accumulates over time. We find ourselves with more wisdom, clarity and strength.

It's Not the Destination but the Journey

Harvey certainly wanted to enjoy the increase in income, prestige and position, as we all do; but the significance is in what he had to shift in himself in order to bring this level of success to fruition. He had to dig deep beyond bible-belt beliefs and family circumstances in order to truly honor his gifts and talents. It required that he recognize all of what he brings to the workplace – just as he's always wanted and provided for others. He had to reframe spiritual tenets to see that it's not about the money or about worthiness; it's about breaking through belief systems that don't serve one's awakening. He had to think outside of a very seductive context in order to realize himself more fully.

Now that he has come to this part of the journey he asks, "What do I have to do to feel comfort and security? For me, personally, I don't see it as a possibility."

I wanted to ask, "Why did you get this raise and position if it wasn't for the comfort and security that comes along with it?" It wasn't a question to be asked out loud, not yet, because to Harvey, there was so much more going on.

Until this moment, the edge of Harvey's comfort zone had been to receive equal payment for the value that he brings to his work. Now that he has expanded his comfort zone to include this, he is once again on the edge of his comfort zone. The question he sits with is "how do I allow myself to enjoy my life, and experience the comfort and security I've created for myself?" This is a brand new world he is opening up to.

There's a point where one realizes there is no end or finish line. Those who pretend otherwise mask physical discomforts that arise when living inside a box, which consistently feels smaller and smaller. What's the point if we never arrive at our final destination – if we never get to fully reap the rewards of our labor? Why not just settle for less – less stress, less effort, less personal abuse?

The questions lead us to ask: What is success? What is fulfillment? What's it all about? If it's not about stuff and winning, then what's worth the effort?

For many people, especially men, the crisis means coming to the edge of one's reality, peering over, and saying, "there's nothing there!" Illnesses, job loss, collapses of the economy all bring us to these same
- moments of realization, which reveal there's no

security, no money, only nothing! What's that about? Big dilemma! Go forward – there's nothing. Stop – and there's nothing.

The reason so many of us choose to not choose is because whatever dilemma we face, choosing to choose brings us to the edge of our comfort zones. It requires that we be uncomfortable; that we see ourselves and our reality differently; and that we explore and experiment with the countless facets of the achievement we've come to be, not have, in this life. The edge of nothing is the same edge as something. The practice of walking both sides of this edge, fearlessly, well, it's pretty darn scary.

Harvey has gone forward, found that it's not about the money, winning or things. He's now onto his next big adventure, knowing that whatever he finds, it won't be about that either. Fortunately he sees the humor in it all and we both laugh our heads off. Being in business is a very fun adventure indeed.

8: Security and the Constant Temptation to Yield to Expediency

Everyone in business desires freedom from worry, and to know that all is secure. Security is a wonderful feeling, which all of us seek yet few of us actually experience fully. Especially with the economic downturn – no one is safe from the potential demise of the current world market.

A year and a half ago, I took myself out of the game, as it were, in order to follow an intuition – a calling onto a trajectory that I knew would reap extraordinary rewards that I had not yet even imagined.

In the tarot cards, the Tower card is one of the twenty-two Major Arcana cards. The image is a large burning tower from which a person falls. Some interpretations say he was thrown off, others say he jumped.

The image basically represents – in my interpretation, the creation of this tower of power, the culmination of belief and material stuff. Standing at its precipice, one is filled with pride of achievement, with worry and concern that it isn't enough, or with disdain that someone is going to take it all away. Or, with a sense of freedom and liberation – now this … what next?

Universal consciousness – the Guy with the proverbial two by four – knocks us upside the head and off we go, over the side of our tower of power. We never know what it will be: Cancer, accidents, relationship endings, or financial crisis. And, we are always surprised when it happens. "I never saw it coming!"

I'm constantly amazed at the degree to which we practice any of the basic tenets of our religious and spiritual traditions. The perennial teachings tell us that we can't find security in the material world – it doesn't exist. They say that through letting go of attachments, being kind and compassionate, generous and accepting, one will inherit the earth. Expounding to others what we ourselves are unwilling to practice is common behavior around the globe. We rarely prepare or ready ourselves for the moment when we are thrown from our tower of power.

Those unique few who jump willingly, know that the adventure isn't in the arrival, the hoarding, the worry and the pride of the accumulation of power. It's in the fall – in the quality of the experience when you are momentarily liberated from what you thought was yours! It's not about being fearful and panicked. It's about getting clear of the values you value most.

A friend of mine, Gary, has owned his own business for the past six years and is feeling the pinch of the economic downturn. He has realized that he's working himself to the bone so that when he retires he can travel and be free. When imagining himself in that place, a certain degree of discomfort arises.

Another friend, Marcy, tells of a wealthy individual who retired early and is now depressed and suicidal. Meanwhile, my friend Carmen found herself catapulted out of her cushy comfort zone, and though she studied spirituality for years, she is shaken and distraught that her life has come to this – she was laid off. Another friend, employed at IBM for eleven years, found himself literally hurled over the rocky edge of a break wall, landing ten feet below with his head inches from a rock that would have ended his life. Consciously he did not jump, yet eyewitnesses say it looked as though he leaped. The fall ended his life as he knew it. The extraordinary circumstances brought about a whole new reality – one that said "Reality – Imagine That!"

Few of us – especially in Western Civilization – have cultivated an awareness of who we are and what we value. We don't know that we don't know, and with blissful ignorance, swim along in the current of the reality we are born into. Even though our holy books are near our bedsides, we pay no attention to our personal relationship with the concepts shared in them.

Jumping from a burning tower – expediency – is the fastest way down, but it may kill you! Staying in the burning building – that too will kill you. You have to choose. Or, to *not* choose means that you abdicate your power and let the Holy Roller cast the dice for you. It's a dilemma!

My own experience of this leap/jump/fall dilemma is that I've come to question my values – even the value of life itself. It's a scary exploration. A large percentage of people die within months of retiring. Their lives seem to have no value once they leave their jobs behind. Work and its stresses gave them a sense of purpose, even though the work itself may have been unfulfilling. At least they could fantasize about what they would do with their lives once they retired and left it all behind. Walking away from their tower of power provided a crisis point, which they all too often found too devastating.

Self-help books, whether psychological or spiritually oriented, encourage us to cultivate a realization that we are not our jobs, our bank accounts, our cars, nor our relationships. We are none of that. We are encouraged to take a serious look at who we really are, what it is we really want and to explore our personal relationship with our spiritual life.

The Dilemma

Making and taking the time to leap/fall/jump reaps rewards you'd never imagine. But in our busy lives, when does one find the time for spiritual practice? Surrendering attachments to the self-importance derived from our availability to others through texts, emails and cell phones, well, that's a lot to be with. With all that we've gained through the gifts of technology, we've also lost our freedom and right to be. We've corrupted our belief system by saying "it's imperative to be available to everyone but myself." We are afraid of who we are in the silence of our own stillness.

I have a theory that "insomnia" is running rampant these days because the middle of the night, when lying in bed, is the only possible time that we can be alone with our own selves. Being alone with ourselves is becoming such a foreign experience, it terrifies us – so, we take medication to numb ourselves in this way as well.

Whether we leap or are pushed from our tower of power, we are faced with the inevitable 'be-with.' All the avoidance strategies we engaged no longer keep us from being in the midst of feeling powerless, helpless and hopeless – foundational human experiences that we spend lifetimes avoiding. To proactively engage with these human experiences as if they were our lovers, would minimize the pain and suffering that we heap onto ourselves by attempting to avoid what is inherent in our humanness.

Because we exist, we are sometimes powerless, helpless and hopeless. Accepting that this is just the way it is liberates us from attempting to avoid it! We can begin then, to laugh, and see how silly we've been to think so highly of ourselves.

9: Putting the Fun Back in Dysfunctional

Dysfunction is a matter of interpretation, isn't it? What is dysfunctional? How do we know if we, or our businesses are dysfunctional? And, what do we do about it?

Dysfunctional families breed individuals who, to some degree, are dysfunctional. And without a doubt, they bring that dysfunction with them into everything they create. They build friendships, careers, and empires around their dysfunction and attract others into their web. At some point, though, as with most empires, they come crashing down. The limitations that come with their dysfunction inevitably destroy what they've created.

Dysfunction essentially means something is working to the detriment of the outcome desired. The degree to which I'm dysfunctional is the degree to which I'm in denial of my dysfunction, and the dysfunction of my organization. When in denial, I'm unwilling to acknowledge responsibility for what's showing up for me or my organization. I blame others for my demise and the demise of my company. I fail, rather than admit and deal with my underlying attachments to family patterns, and to the secret world that's hidden inside me. I am unwilling to risk losing what I consider to be rightfully mine for the sake of the business, my investors and employees. I'll take it all down with me, rather than lose face with myself. This is dysfunction!

On the other hand, we may have come from the most supportive and loving families possible – ones we consider highly functioning. These highly functioning families have some important dynamics in place: Open communication, respect for individual needs and desires, a sense of humor, safety and trust, a capacity to admit when one is wrong, open to outside support, and boundaries that provide healthy limits while encouraging openness to expansion and change. At the same time, every healthy family provides limiting patterns and beliefs, which at some point will be to the detriment of the individual member. Funny how that works. Even the healthiest of families can't make it all right.

I've just been hired by a company in Kansas City, to work with a number individuals who are important – even vital to the project at hand, yet bring behavior patterns that, if not shifted, will devastate their current project and consequently the entire organization.

In a preliminary meeting with HR, I questioned the degree to which the company itself and the executives running it were willing to look at their own contribution to what's occurring with their employees. I described how, quite often, employees act out much like children in a family. Too often, parents will send their children to therapy, but won't go themselves; though parents are actually the ones generating the dysfunctional environment in which the children live and operate. Unless the parents come into therapy, the environment will remain the same and the children will either revert to old patterns, or, having cultivated healthier dynamics, may choose to leave. So, with regard to this company that has just employed me, it will mostly need coaching too, if it really wants fulfillment and success.

Parents who lose their children to Social Services do so because they can't manage and be responsible for their little creations. Similarly, I know tons of organizations that have had to fire their founders because they were interfering with the growth and development of the vision they created. And, I know even more organizations whose success is limited by the dysfunction of the business and the humans that run it.

Every family system generates some level of enmeshment. Think of a fish not knowing itself separate from the water it swims in. It doesn't matter how this enmeshed system developed, what it's about or how it functions. What matters is cultivating an environment that allows for the process of de-enmeshment. This empowers individuals to differentiate themselves and grow a greater capacity to choose to choose what they choose in service to their own well-being and the fullest expression of Self. And, hopefully, also to the organization they work for.

It doesn't matter what sort of organization we are talking about – an individual, family, small business or the largest corporations, religions, and governments. We are dealing with the process of distinguishing individuals from patterns that limit their growth potential and the growth potential of the organizations they serve.

Companies fail, I believe, because individuals are actually not invested enough in the success they are attempting to achieve. So, it's not that they are truly failing. They succeed at maintaining the environment that generates the undesired outcome, which appears as failure. This sounds paradoxical, however it's what all of us do, consistently, until we wake up to the fact that we are creating our own demise.

When we can see this from a logical perspective, it becomes a no-brainer to choose to think differently. We can cultivate a way of being that creates an environment to generate the outcome we want. It's not a big, hairy monster deal to take the steps to make this happen. It actually becomes fun and very rewarding.

The Dilemma

What's at stake, on one hand, can be the revealing of hidden agendas, survival mechanisms, and alliances that we may not even know we possess. What's also at stake is the project, the business, investors' confidence and money, as well as your reputation; all sorts of circumstantial elements that we are clearly attached to. This is not an either/or proposition. It all has to be explored, revealed, recognized and acknowledged, and it all has to be dealt with openly, with respect, trust, commitment to the vision of the outcome desired, and a large measure of humor.

What I love about working with companies and organizations is that the people at the table are powerful, intelligent, high-stakes players. The outcome of the choices they make are life-changing for themselves and everyone invested in them. Retraining their dysfunctional survival mechanisms to more functional strategies will provide unimaginable success in their projects and careers, if that's what they truly want. (Knowing that somewhere around 80% of all new businesses fail, you've got to wonder what it is they truly want!)

10: Dilemmas Faced by Sole-Proprietors

Many of my clients are individuals who are starting their own business. Like my corporate clients, they continually face a multitude of dilemmas.

The most challenging dilemma for this group is actually committing to the belief that what they have to offer is of value to others, and that they can make a living doing what they love. They worry about the financial prospects and ask themselves time and time again, "Can I make a living doing this? I really want to and I think I can be successful, but …" For many, this *but* is the beginning of the end.

I Really Want to Do This

As a coach, I often have to stop my client after those six words. When they continue with the *but…*, they will only disempower themselves. They focus not on what they want, but on what they don't want: what they don't want to do, what they don't want to happen, what they don't want to be responsible for, what they don't want to lose, and a plethora of consequences, which befall any individual beginning a new venture.

We desire what we desire, and we strive to avoid what is undesirable. That's a no brainer. However more often than not, individuals in the beginning phase of a business startup will withhold their energy because the fear of potentially engaging the undesirable is just too scary. "I don't want to lose what I don't want to lose!"

As you've read through each narrative of this book, you've probably realized that dilemmas pit an individual's desire to fulfill a dream against a fear of loss: loss of dignity, money, property, security, stability; on and on. For too many of us, our motto is "Security at All Cost." Whether it's an individual employed at a large or small company, or the person is self-employed, the choice is always the same: Do I choose based on my fears or do I choose based on my truest desire to bring my best into practice?

I've spent the majority of the past ten years training coaches, and I've loved it. The greatest challenge for me has been to cultivate, in these burgeoning entrepreneurs, the same wisdom that they will have to bring to their own clients. However, they too get caught in their dilemmas, unable to move beyond a limited sense of self. Their capacity to empower people to empower themselves and others is impeded by "But what if I can't …"

In graduate schools, too, the success of highly accredited individuals is often squashed by the lack of self-worth and respect for their own gifts, which they've worked so hard to cultivate. Doesn't it make you crazy when you see individuals, months away from graduating, bail out because they just can't face the potential risks? They'd rather play small than truly engage the experiment of being fully present on the extraordinary adventure they embarked upon years before.

Self-worth is pivotal in any individual realizing their dreams. My experience is that most of us have to step forward, believing in what we have to offer, regardless of the fear that we just may not be good enough. Regardless of the degree of mastery, each of us will be challenged to bring our best to the forefront.

The funny thing is, many of these individuals have such apprehension about starting their business that they continually *not do* what would have them be successful. They can't give themselves the opportunity to fail or to succeed.

In much of the literature around today, there's still the question of passion over payments. Whether corporate, small business or entrepreneur, cultivating one's life work is still based on the old paradigm: You win or you lose. At the same time, there is a rapid increase in visibility of research that supports a new paradigm – one that strongly suggests we create our reality through the beliefs and interpretations we live by. So much of our lives are based on thoughts we don't even know we are thinking.

This new paradigm suggests that we reject our fear-based thinking and instead, take action based on what we know to be true – rather than what we fear to be true.

My clients are required to think differently: only allowing thoughts in support of what they say they want. Too much of what goes through our brains turns out to be ridiculous nonsense. Learning to think differently requires mindfulness – being present to the thoughts that run nonstop. We must train ourselves to carefully choose thoughts that serve our highest and best interests, while rejecting thoughts that take us into a trance-like state, where we forget what we wanted.

What all of us yearn for is to make our highest and best contribution in service to a better world. But what we find when we take a good look at the majority of our thoughts, is that we are immersed in fear-based chatter, which leads us further away from our passions and dreams.

Sole proprietors have to believe in themselves like no one else. Everything is on the line – no buts about it! And, at the same time, they are just like the rest of us who have to choose, day in and day out, how to bring our fullest expression of our essential self into the world.

11: The Personal is the Professional

Being in business, regardless of the position or title, brings us face-to-face with choice-points. It's nonstop! Exploring what has us choose what we choose gets us closer to what motivates us to be who we 'be' and do what we do. It clarifies why our professional and personal lives are what they are and not something different. It explains why, regardless of our ambition, education and experience, we are where we are.

If there were only one thing I'd like to get across to all of my corporate clients, it's that the personal is the professional and the professional is the personal. How we 'be' in our personhood, our humanity and life in general is how we 'be' in our professional world as well. Always, and everywhere.

Within any organization's walls, how one chooses what they choose to choose is most likely how they choose to choose in every other context of their lives. Though the content may be different, the process by which they choose is consistent across the board.

We choose based on some fundamental principles, though these principles will differ from person to person. They are:

•"This is how it's always been done, so that's what I'm choosing to choose now." Limiting parameters restrict our ability to choose to think outside our comfort zone. We can't choose differently because we don't know that we have a choice. We aren't even aware that there is a box to think ourselves out of.

•We are afraid of what others may find out or decide about us. More people than you can imagine operate from this principle. We source our identity from a decision we made a long time ago – perhaps when we were only four years old. At that time, we found ourselves inadequate to bring about conditions we saw as vital, given the context of our little lives. With this assessment of our limitations comes the fear that we will be found inadequate, unworthy and unlovable, humiliated and rejected. At this point, we begin cultivating survival strategies around other people's wants and needs that allow us to avoid being humiliated or rejected. Based on our own interpretations (as a four year old), we go about fulfilling those wants and needs.

Again, more people than you can imagine limit their professional development because they operate from an immature emotional guidance system. This strategy keeps them choosing based on fear, as opposed to the fulfillment of their human spirit. People with greater degrees of emotional intelligence choose based on the needs of the organizations, not fear.

If I continue to choose from a fear-based paradigm, which I developed when I was four years old, I imagine I'll remain safe and invulnerable to attack. The consequence of this choice is that I also can't have what I want, because I'm limiting how I will choose to choose what I choose. If I choose differently, I open myself up to vulnerability. However, I'm more likely to cultivate the capacity to weather attacks, and not be devastated by them. I cannot grow myself professionally and I can't grow the company if I continue to operate from a belief that I made up as a child.

•It's all about me! It's not uncommon to hear my clients say: "Though I said I was a team player and joined this company to further its growth, I'm really only in it for my own personal gain. I choose to choose based on what will bring the highest visibility to my efforts and will get me the promotions I'm seeking."

•I choose to pretend to be a team player, listening for what others want. However, I don't contribute any new ideas for fear of being found out that I'm inadequate. I hate to be ridiculed, so I avoid any possibility of that happening, even if it means not getting promoted. In this way, I gain asylum from ridicule and feeling inadequate.

Frankly, we are all in it for personal gain. However, this can mean different things to different people. Personal gain can be related to security, stability and safety, to gaining recognition and rewards, to gaining freedom, fun and flexibility. We never know what personal gain means to us until we distinguish what it is that we want from our life in general, and our professional life, specifically.

•Healthier individuals will ask: What's in the best interest of the organization and in my best interest at the same time? A client may say: "I can see my own limitations and inadequacies, and based on the fear of being found out I can hide in other peoples' vision, and limit the fulfillment of my personal and professional vision. At the same time, I know that there are ways of being that will advance the initiatives I believe in. In alignment with those initiatives, I'm willing to open myself to possibility, as well as risk ridicule. I will be assertive with my opinions and ideas, though this may risk appearing inadequate. I'm willing to be expansive in cultivating my repertoire of possibility, though this may lead to being seen as ungrounded and unstable.

What needs to be in place in order to support a breakthrough of this dilemma? Trust!

Trust is foundational to any change process. If you don't trust the organization, your execs, managers, or even your peers, then you won't choose to choose differently – it's too risky! If you don't trust yourself to have what it takes – an adequate amount of skills, experience, knowledge, and most importantly, self-trust, then you won't take even baby steps toward your desired goal.

Just as an experiment, notice where there is a choice-making process occurring in both your personal and professional life. Perhaps, for example, you'll notice that how you speak to your direct reports is the same way you speak to your children or your partner. This can be a fascinating exploration, and will contribute to your capacity to choose in alignment with what you really want.

12: Every Choice-point Grows Leadership

Leaders aren't made by titles, position, or prestige. They are made by the choices they make throughout their career, which at the time seem to have nothing to do with becoming a leader. It has only to do with a person's current situation throwing curve balls, requiring them to make choices that are in the highest good of the company and in their own highest truth as well.

Let's say that the company you work for is challenged on many fronts. They are not fulfilling specific agreements, which had initially enticed you to join the organization. You still believe in the product and service, but no longer trust the competence of the leaders to generate what's required for your success. Given the current situation, you feel powerless to make a difference for yourself or the company.

You saw yourself rising in the ranks to a level of leadership where you'd make a difference in how the company functions and fulfills its vision. You looked forward to the responsibility that came with the title and position. You want to make a difference, however, in this moment, you are asking yourself why you work for a company that seems chaotic, disorganized and off-course.

Though you've seen yourself on this trajectory towards leadership, currently you feel stuck, with no clue how to choose what's next for you. You feel as though your future may have been stolen from you and now you are at the mercy of this company to make choices that will hopefully impact in positive ways. Should you go or should you stay? What to do?

Too often we look at the situations we find ourselves in and feel disempowered, disappointed and perhaps depressed. We've trusted our company to make choices that will reward us personally and professionally. What happens when the company fails to make choices that lead to healthy development of the organization itself, its bottom line and employees – you in particular?

Leadership development takes place in the present moment – now! The challenges you currently face are the very elements that are required for leadership capacities to be cultivated. And, the choices you make now, regardless of your current level of power, have a huge influence on the company. It's rather funny how we miss this point.

We think that the trajectory to leadership is one thing and when we arrive we will have what it takes to lead. However, it doesn't occur to us that we actually have to develop muscles of leadership somewhere along the way. Learning theories in trainings, books and MBAs aren't the same as having to actualize those theories in real business situations. Every good leader learns to walk their talk through countless moments of uncertainty. They've learned which muscles are required for each specific situation. They've strengthened and stretched those muscles – and others they were yet conscious of, in order to be the leader they've become.

Leadership is an evolutionary process. Every confronting situation builds a repertoire of skills. Over time, those skills feel natural and intuitive, as though you've always had what it takes.

The process of choice-making is the essential element of leadership. How you choose to be, given the circumstances of this current moment, is very telling. Being present to the dilemmas that face the company and you – personally and professionally, is the point where great leaders are born. They are born, not by their employers or their promotions; they actually birth themselves through every choice-point they meet.

Every one of these choice-points has to be met with a level of presence to one's personal and professional investment, while keeping the organization's needs and requirements in mind. These dilemmas can be very weighing. Great leaders intentionally cultivate their capacity to lead through each situation they meet. They distinguish all the variables at play, then discern what's in the best interest of the company at large, which includes themselves.

In the previous chapter, The Personal is the Professional, we explored how every choice made by every employee is personal and at the same time professional. Some choices we face are good for us but not for the company. Sometimes the choices we make are good for the company and not for us. Some are good for neither the company nor us, and what good leaders are able to discern is how to choose so that the highest good is attained for all.

Every situation provides opportunities to grow leadership capacities. The consequence of bypassing challenging or confronting relationships and situations is that you miss opportunities to cultivate the very skills required to be the leader you see yourself to be.

You might be expressing frustration right now because you think you don't know how to cultivate what's required to be in your current situation, other than frustrated, powerless and incapable of change. I encourage you – and your organization, to bring in a thinking partner – a coach or mentor to empower all of you to look at your situations differently. Doing so allows you to see the choice-point you are currently engaged in and what's required to choose most effectively as a leader for your own development and for your company as well.

Choices made from integrity and accountability will always be in the highest good of all involved. Every moment will provide opportunities to cultivate your leadership capacities. Be curious about yourself and notice opportunities to experiment with different ways of being. Today is the day to step into the leadership role you see as yours.

13: Losing Makes Us Winners

Because of the choices we've made throughout our lives, there will come a time when no matter what, it will feel as if all will be lost. In this moment we experience a shattering. Our dreams of a life that felt stable and safe disappear. Perhaps all our possessions are lost or taken away. In times like this, we do one of two things: we blame ourselves for the choices we've made, for our incompetence and inadequacies that got us into this mess. Or, we blame others for the choices they've made, for their incompetence and their inadequacies that got us into this mess. Betrayed, abandoned, alone and lost, feeling powerless, hopeless and helpless; in these moments, we hate being human!

Be Afraid – Be Very Afraid

Hurricanes, tsunamis, economic downturns, misuse of power, accidents, layoffs - you get the picture. Our dearest treasures, be it possessions, people, our identities, youth, beauty – our lives – somehow, someday, it all gets taken away.

I spoke to a group of individuals who not too long ago were laid off or fired from their management and executive positions in Silicon Valley. What was revealed was that they experienced elements of trauma and tragedy in having their positions and livelihoods taken away. Houses repossessed, bankruptcy, plummeting self-worth and self-respect. What would be the point in rebuilding any of it, they asked. It will all be taken away again.

The intention of my talk with this group of unemployed San Francisco residents was to engage them in a deeper listening to themselves. I wanted them to excavate this one, single moment of dire disappointment and shattered dreams. Through this uncovering, the likelihood of also revealing outmoded beliefs could allow them to choose to grieve what had been lost, and then choose differently in service to personal and professional fulfillment.

Such deep listening brings one to a dilemma. If they hear, see and reflect upon what they believed to be true, prior to their *fall from grace,* then they would have to prioritize their numerous values, and sit in discernment to make sense of it all. What to keep, what to let go of, and what no longer serves their highest good & their highest truth? With everything taken away, what is one left with? And if, through discernment, these individuals find that everything they worked for amounted to a hill of beans – then what? They would have to let go, and grieve the loss of what didn't really matter in the first place. YUCK!

On the other hand, if any one of these participants chose to decide to remain a victim to their circumstances, then they have chosen a disempowered path for themselves. They will have no way out of what looks like a pretty empty and unfulfilling catastrophe. Here too, they will have to let go of and grieve the loss of what didn't really matter in the first place. YUUUCKKK!

As discussed in Chapter 8, regarding our Tower of Power, I shared how I chose to leap instead of being thrown from my tower. Thinking my outstretched wings would have me soar, instead I plummeted, not realizing my wings had yet to fully form. I lost just about everything, which was a chance I took. And, over time I've been discovering that my *fall from grace* was not as foolish as it first seemed. Unearthing lifetimes of themes labeled *This Too Was Taken Away From Me,* led me to witness how, in the past, I clung with white knuckles to the idea that I could actually keep life from sliding into a dismal cataclysm. I saw how I've kept myself rather small in service to minimizing the amount I would or could lose once again.

Many of my nights are spent in deep conversation with myself and my God, discerning what is reality, really. I unveil the many ways I contributed to life turning out the way it has, as opposed to how I imagined it to be. Part of me is so angry that I have failed to bring about the fulfillment of the fairytale happily-ever-after. This rageful aspect in me blames me for not living up to its expectations. It brings up, time and time again, the degree to which I am inadequate and incompetent. In the midst of this bludgeoning, I want to die, just to end this process that seems to have no end.

The only analogy I have that is comparable to this process is having the flu – one that requires enormous amount of vomiting to rid the body of the toxic virus. Though you've purged yourself far more than you ever imagined possible, you still retrieve elements from within and wonder "Where the heck did that come from?" Last night was no different for me, as I purged out the phrase: "How could you let this happen? You are so incompetent!"

This time, I listened to my own verbal abuse and thought "Wow, you've been doing this your whole life." Then I asked this righteous, angry part of myself (better known as my ego), "Why are you so angry? You too played a role in the circumstances being what they are. We are here, together, in this human experience. Get over it, and let's look at this differently so we can see our stumbling blocks."

Well, the conversation turned around for the better. Staying in this deep, empty space, I discovered that I decided a long time ago that I didn't want to have it all taken away again. So, I'd play it safe by playing small; all the while working really hard to have the life I say I want. I also acknowledged that everyone loses everything, sooner or later. This brings us to a choice-point where we decide what is worth losing. I might as well take a job that requires no personal risk, if I'm not willing to lose what I've been afraid to lose all along. That is, my belief in my ability to make a huge contribution to the betterment of the world.

The Vase is Already Broken

Just like every individual at my talk in San Francisco, I have two choices. I can avoid losing, thus minimizing risk while minimizing fulfillment. Or, I do what I love, enjoy the exploration and experiment of being me, here, now, inching my way towards my highest and best contribution to the world. In this moment I can choose to do what I love, knowing, in actual fact, that there is nothing to lose and only a human experience to gain. It's a time filled with wonder and unknowns, available only by choosing once again to fling myself off my Tower of Power.

I believe we came into our humanness to experience all of it – the highs and the lows, the agony and the ecstasy. I believe too that we've chosen the themes and the characters we play, so as to experience what this aspect of life is like and to grow and develop into wiser individuals. Losing actually makes us winners!

14: Freedom's Just Another Word for ...

Yoda says, "Train yourself to let go of everything you fear to lose." Wow! Think about what that would look like in the business world: Letting go of winning, power, promotions and bonuses; being right and other people being wrong; complaining, blaming and shaming; stress and worry and all the underlying reasons for the stress and worry. What would you be left with?

Susan is an artist working for a national corporation. She's been with the company just over eight years and from the beginning has struggled with her place in her team, and in her department. The environment feels confusing and frustrating because, no matter what, she feels isolated, criticized and marginalized by her team and boss. She sought me out for coaching because of the degree to which she was experiencing physical and emotional exhaustion after giving her all to a project. Her team is about to embark on a similar project and she's facing the same dilemma. This time, she's conscious that it's not just her physical health on the line; she feels it's her soul that will be ripped away from her forever.

Susan is married with a five-year old daughter. Her income is important to sustaining a moderate lifestyle in the Boulder Area. She feels powerless to be effective and begins to sob, feeling like a failure to make anything different.

"What options do you have, Susan?" I asked, after the tears subsided. She shared how things were exactly as they had been many months ago, even after new managers and bosses replaced the old regime. Matter-of-factly, she responds: "I have no options." "Really?" I ask. "There are no options?" "Yes, there are no options," she continued: "except to keep my mouth shut and my head down and do what I am told. But I know that means setting myself up for an emotional and physical breakdown, and that's not an option!"

"There are other options," I countered. "Are you up for taking a look at them?"

What I was attempting to get across to Susan was that one of her options was to leave the company and go somewhere that may offer her a more workable situation for her. Because of her need for income, she didn't see leaving as an option. Nor did she see that letting go of everything she feared to lose was an option. Susan's perspective offered no option. She was in a hopeless stalemate.

Yoda also said: "A Jedi must have the deepest commitment, the most serious mind." What does that mean, in Susan's situation? By having the deepest commitment and the most serious mind, it's easier to fully align with your true commitments. In Susan's case, she is committed to her personal and professional success, and maintaining her reputation as an artist. (She fears that if she leaves the company her reputation will be further tarnished.)

Something else Susan is committed to is keeping healthy – it's not an option to sell her soul to the devil again. Yet, through my eyes, it looks very much like this is happening. When someone as brilliant as Susan gives herself no options, she's a sitting duck. She's already giving her soul away.

Each of us has been trained to see the world in a specific way. In many families, communities and business environments, it's essential to our survival to maintain the status quo. So, we maintain that perspective, no matter what, even though it may be harmful to our well-being. However, our minds can't make sense of our reality if it no longer looks the way it's *supposed* to. Much like Susan, we are each faced, at times, with no options and no way to move forward, except to do what we've done in the past. This often precipitates depression, despair, as well as interesting diseases, ailments and unanticipated calamities.

If we don't want to lose what we are afraid of losing, our egoic self will bend and twist reality in such a way that we experience "stuckness." We can feel lost in the midst of bright lights and crowds of people. It's not uncommon for individuals to experience mental and emotional exhaustion and breakdown. Inevitably they lose more than they were bargaining for, because it's too scary to look at options that may alienate them from others or from the ways it's *always* been. Aren't we a curious species?

Susan faces this specific dilemma because she has a great deal at stake. On the one hand, she has her position, her credibility and all she's invested in her career, which she fears could go down the toilet in a heartbeat. On the other hand, her physical, mental, emotional and spiritual health is steadily deteriorating.

75

She's unable to be attentive to her daughter and husband the way she would like to be. Yet attempting to hang on to what she's got will most likely mean she'll lose everything. This sounds crazy, but it's the way it works.

Train yourself to let go of everything you fear to lose

Where Susan sees no options, I see she has no options too, but from a different perspective. Unless she opens herself up to the possibilities she currently doesn't want to see, she *will* lose everything. My job as her coach is to gently steward her towards what now appears to be too frightening to accept. Inevitably, she will have to choose to shift her paradigm and begin to accept a reality she doesn't yet believe exists.

Freedom's just another word for "nothing left to lose"

For some, this process is a walk in the park. For others, it can be experienced as a shattering. There's nothing wrong with a shattering. A shattering is the same as a paradigm shift; it's just far more challenging in every way imaginable. And, generally speaking, it takes a great deal more time to recover.

What's right in front of Susan is right in front of each and every one of us: the opportunity to discover what's worth losing and what's not. It all goes away, eventually. In this moment, though, it's just a matter of choosing to choose to be accountable and responsible for the consequence of the choices Susan has to make. I hate this part as much as anyone else. I want it all good and easy. When it's not, I don't want to look at options that terrify me. I've learned, though, that my life isn't worth living if fear is the only conductor on the train.

I'm listening to Yoda and other spiritual teachers in order to create a life worth living. In time, Susan will begin to cultivate courage – enough to see the many options in front of her. She will discern for herself, from her heart and soul, which options serve her highest good and her highest truth.

15: In Pursuit of Mei-Li

Mei-Li has a Ph.D. and works for one the biggest communication companies in the world. Originally from China, she has been in Silicon Valley, California for the majority of her adult life. Married with two children, Mei-Li is very happy. However, she has been facing a challenging dilemma for many years: Though she is happy, successful and fulfilled in her life, she's concerned that she should do more – be more.

Mei-Li observes her boss focusing most of his attention on getting ahead. She sees other women at her level of management working for that next promotion, that next level of leadership and responsibility. "I don't want an increase in responsibility – I don't want to work that hard. I don't like talking with people as much as I'd need to, to move to the next level of management. But, shouldn't I want to? Is there something wrong with me that I don't want to do that? I'm afraid there's something very wrong with me."

As Mei-Li shares with me over many coaching sessions, I coach her to see the dilemma she is currently constrained by. On the one hand, Mei-Li loves her job and the team she manages. She has the free time she needs to be available to her children and husband. She isn't stressed and unnerved by unmet deadlines. She's actually one of the 10% of the workforce that feels fulfilled in her career.

On the other hand, Mei-Li's culture, married with our Western culture, attempts to move people into work that isn't theirs to do. Mei-Li watches people spend more time being people-pleasers than effective employees and she finds this frustrating and confusing. "People aren't getting their work done while they are schmoozing for a promotion. Should I be doing that? The fact is, I don't like schmoozing. I don't like going to cocktail parties, playing golf or any of those other social things that you are supposed to do if you want to get ahead. I'm a pretty reclusive person who enjoys my life the way it is. But I feel like I should be doing more."

Many of us face this dilemma of being more – doing more; and at the same time, we have the fulfillment we want in what we are doing right now. Aren't we supposed to want more money and power? Aren't we supposed to want the bigger office and more schmoozing time with influential people?

My sense is, and I shared this with Mei-Li in our session, that what people want is to get to a place where there is fulfillment in their work and personal life – that there is balance with health and happiness. I believe that most people want what Mei-Li already has. The current within the corporate structure drags many people like Mei-Li into its undertow toward some fantasy life that is wrought with a lot of what they don't want. There are few who willingly choose health and fulfillment with what they have, what they do and how they 'be.'

Mei-Li laughs as she begins to see a bigger picture – one that allows her free choice to choose for herself what's hers to do. She laughs to hear that what people are struggling for is what she already has. She laughs as she realizes that she is presently free to choose to be happy in the life she has created and if in the future she feels inspired to grow her career toward greater degrees of leadership and responsibility, she can do that.

Mei-Li isn't out of the undertow, and as long as she is in the corporate environment there will always be that current of influence. The degree to which she can stay committed to her well-being and fulfillment in her career, the less pull all of this will have on her.

Mei-Li has found an eddy. for now, where she is out of the stream of influence of others. She is finding herself – the one she believes she has to continually pursue. It takes strength and courage to step out of the normal way of being for the sake of what we are all striving for: well-being and fulfillment in our careers. It's kind of crazy when you think about it! Perhaps the pursuit of Mei-Li has come to a happy ending; right here where she has been, but now enjoying it to a much larger degree!

16: It's All Happening in this Moment

After seven years at the same corporation, Will, a manager for a Silicon Valley manufacturing company, wants out! He has a plan that will unfold over the next five years, but with a third child on the way, a new house and mortgage in a trendy, expensive neighborhood, he has to stay put. He just doesn't know how he'll be able to stand it!

What's so bad about Will's current position, you might ask? Well, he has a new boss whose ineffective management style is demoralizing for Will and his team. This guy has taken the fun out every moment of Will's day. On top of that, there are a couple of fellows who, if not micromanaged by Will, just won't get the work done. He feels as though he has to keep the pressure on them to perform. Will also feels the pressure of the corporate environment to be competitive and always look good. He's overwhelmed, stressed and exhausted by all of this and more. And he isn't able to do what he was actually hired to do. It's Crazy!

As Will imagines going forward with his new vision, and at the same time staying put in his current position, he begins to suffer anxiety attacks. He's also experiencing confusion. He's been in the corporate environment for 15 years and now he's seriously considering a move out of that world to something his rational mind can't make sense of – it feels suicidal. To his egoic self, it is suicide.

On the one hand, Will has a commitment to his family, his boss, his team and his company. And, he is experiencing a deep commitment to follow through with what feels like a calling – something compelling him to get out of this straightjacket of a career. He doesn't know another way to make a living and yet, he is faced with this part of himself that can no longer engage in the day-to-day efforting of his job. He wants out, and at the same time, he can't afford to quit.

Will envisions himself a speaker and lecturer – inspiring people to live lives that are fulfilling. He wants to encourage and empower people to take the leap of faith. Now he finds himself standing at that very precipice. In this moment he has to walk his talk.

Through our coaching conversation, Will reveals that within his current position he has plenty of opportunities to take those leaps of faith and to walk his talk. Letting go of specific mechanisms, which he's counted on throughout his career requires him to step into the unknown – again, the very destination he will encourage others to travel to.

Will is smart and wise. He easily sees what he has in store for himself. He laughs at the dilemma he's got himself in, and knows what he has to do. That doesn't make it easier, but seeing what's ahead and what he'll need to practice is a good start.

Part of Will's practice will be to deal with his anxiety in a much more empowered way. Part of our discussion is about how anxiety keeps us from stepping off into dangerous territory.

This Moment – Now!

The moment we find ourselves in – right now, is. It is clean and clear of everything except for what we bring to it. In this moment we can witness and observe, without any contribution of thought or interpretation. However, 99.9% of the time, we contaminate the moment with thoughts of hopes and fear, bringing about somatic responses, such as anxiety, stress, and nervous tension. This moment is generally taken up with thinking about the past or the future. At least 70% of our thoughts are negative. All of those thoughts are happening now, in this moment – because that is all we have – this moment! We alone bring thoughts to this moment that will precipitate anxiety.

I use the analogy of riding a bicycle as an adult. Let's say you haven't ridden a bike in ten years, and you are about to put your foot on the pedal, when you remember the number of times you fell off your bike as a kid. You remember all of the times you bloodied your knees, elbows and head. You begin to feel scared and decide it's too risky. Bad things happened in the past, so bad things can happen in this moment. You climb off the bike and give it back to your eight-year-old daughter.

Well, the same process occurs regarding anxiety, except that the memories of failure or danger are much deeper in our unconscious. We can't access the source of anxiety as easily as we can the memories of falling off our bike. So, we assume that it must be this moment that is the source of the anxiety. Again, this moment is free of all that stuff except for what we bring to it.

By grasping this small but significant truth, Will began to think differently, which allowed him to consider different ways of being in relation to this present moment and to anxiety.

As he masters this practice of being in this moment and distinguishing any and all thoughts he brings to it, he will begin to recognize the very thoughts that have him hate his job and want to leave. He'll cultivate awareness of what has him so unfulfilled and be able to see that all of it – ALL OF IT – is made up of thoughts he's dragged in with him. Consciously he'll begin to choose differently in service to the calling that will take him far beyond his current dilemma.

Like Will, each of us experiences overwhelm, anxiety and confusion when we find ourselves at the crossroads of change. Emptying this moment of thoughts that no longer contribute to our well-being, frees us to practice something different – effortlessly!

17: No Peace on Earth

There will never be peace on Earth. Never! Not as long as humans put themselves in charge of right and wrong, good and bad, prosperity and poverty. Nope: It ain't gonna happen!

Peace will come when we give up doing unto ourselves and others what is hurtful, harmful and destructive. I drink coffee and alcohol, use sugar and eat meat and wheat – all of which are destructive to my system. I use electronics, drive a fossil-fueled vehicle and count on many organizations that contribute to the destruction of the planet, to keep me safe and comfortable. Like the majority of individuals on the planet, as I mentioned earlier, 70% of my thoughts are negative. This also contributes to an internal environment that is not peace-full; it is actually dis-eased. I've been in relationships with people that cause me constant frustration, and my expectations have me distance myself, withdraw and withhold. I feel victimized and want to get back at individuals who've broken promises and ignored agreements. Yet, I say I want peace.

I have come to realize that the world doesn't need fixing – no peace required. It is perfect and faultless in providing an environment within which we learn and grow through the trials and tribulations of the circumstances we are presented with. That is the whole deal with coming into human form and to Earth University. Make all the classes easy and effortless and the learning disappears. Therefore, we need the world the way it is, until we need it another way, and then, it will miraculously become that!

From the perspective of the Domain of Universal Oneness, all corporations and business environments are also perfect for getting the learning we need. Perfection is always and everywhere. It's up to us to get smart enough to recognize such perfection and utilize it for the very purpose for which it's presented.

My perspective, in this moment, is that we are here, enrolled in Earth School – from nursery school to post-graduate work. We are here to become enlightened to greater and greater degrees. There is no end to which one can become enlightened; learning opportunities just keep on coming. It's as if the more conscious and enlightened we become the more the Universe creates a greater array of challenges for our species. Eckhart Tolle said that never before could a species consciously choose evolution. Evolution: Hmmmmm. Is there ever an end to evolution? I dare say there is none!

How do we evolve? We evolve only when we are at the edge of our comfort zone and are pushed or voluntarily push that edge to include what never before was possible, what could never be imagined and, what is now only a twinkle in our Creator's eye! There is no limit to our evolution as long as we keep ourselves in the game.

Okay, so that sounds as if we can take ourselves out of the game. No, we can't. And you may think you want to because the game in some ways seems to be getting bigger than you, and scarier than you planned on. It may be; however, that's what's important to focus on, given the current circumstance: what's yours to do. What Course are you currently in and what are the objectives of this particular learning opportunity? No, you can't take yourself out of the game, because, like the Dali Lama's hot dog, you are one with everything.

I believe that most of us have some investment in saving the planet – that somewhere in our personal or professional vision, there's a compelling desire to make this world a better place for all. In the world of business, it's no different. Yet, we are challenged to do the job we are hired to do, at the same time attempting to cultivate an environment that is healthier to work in. At times we throw up our hands and whine, "Is there no peace?"

As I began, so I shall complete with "No, probably not." This doesn't mean that life will be full of despair, frustration and depression – not any more than it has been up until now. So, learn to be peaceful within, though the circumstances around you are not to your liking. Find what causes a lack of peace, and ask yourself what would be valuable to learn, discover or practice in situations within which you feel out of control. This is how you cultivate peace – at least for moments at a time.

A couple of years ago, I retired from saving the Earth and all the people and beings that live here too. Sometimes I forget that I retired. But, when I remember, it's clear that what's mine and only mine to do is: to let myself off the hook for being human, less than perfect, not fulfilling other people's expectations, and to stop feeling guilty and shameful about my inadequacies and unworthiness. What's mine to do is to practice kindness and to be mindful of what I do that could be harmful, while minimizing my impact on the earth.

I love peaceful moments and pray that all of us can share peace – if only for moments at a time. They are exquisite!

18: Ineptness as a Masterful Teacher

Hank is a young fellow working for a fifteen-year-old company in Sarasota, Florida. He is frustrated because there is a lack of momentum on the part of his manager to fully implement Hank's gifts and skills. He's frustrated because he feels underutilized and unfulfilled. He feels like a racehorse that isn't given enough rein to really run the race and win. He's being held back, but why?

More often than not, managers aren't conscious of how they influence their team. They don't even know that there's a way they are being that limits the success of their direct reports and the company as well. Sometimes, they hold back their direct reports in service to their own desired outcomes. Usually, they just don't know what they are doing.

What Hank hears from his boss is to not push for change too quickly; "Things take time around here. Slow and steady wins the race." Hank isn't a tortoise; he's a thoroughbred. He was hired for his expertise and the results he's capable of. He has the passion and capability to make things happen quickly. After two years with this company under this particular manager, Hank has exhausted much of his creative energies fighting his manager for more free rein.

Hank's Dilemma:

Hank's dilemma isn't foreign at all to many individuals working under a management style that holds them back rather than supporting growth and expansion. How does he bring the best he can to a situation where his manager really doesn't know how to manage a thoroughbred like Hank? He could quit; however, is there something else that's happening here for Hank that could bring value to his time in this company? What's possible here as a learning opportunity?

Through our coaching, Hank gets clearer that he is being exposed to a management style that is ineffective for him and people like him. He wants things to change. He wants his manager to be more of a mentor; he wants to move up in the ranks and be a leader himself in bigger and better ways. He's stuck behind a plow horse and can't see his way clear to run the race he believes he is here to win.

A fascinating aspect of Hank's dilemma is that he is actually in a perfect internship opportunity to learn to be a really good leader for people like himself. Rather than focus on how ineffective his manager is, he can focus on two things: 1) What's missing in his manager's style that if it were present would spur Hank on to greater success? 2) What's available in the current situation that can be of benefit to him and his leadership development? What's incubating within him that will bring about a much more powerful leadership style?

I believe these questions are so essential in business coaching. Sometimes our clients can't change their circumstance; however they can shift their perspective. I believe that every situation we find ourselves in is an internship – a place to learn what we need to learn.

More often than not, like Hank, we didn't consciously sign up for these learning opportunities. Thoroughbreds want to run – they don't want to do anything else – there's nothing else to do but get to the finish line. However, Hank has an opportunity to learn and take notes on how to be a leader who is committed to the best and highest contribution of his team. He can only do this through his current experience.

Being fully immersed in his current circumstance, Hank is having an experience that informs him of his own personal reality, needs and desires; of what capacities he sees that are required to work in this type of environment; and, of what capacities he wants to cultivate to be the manager he wishes he had for himself, and that he wants to be for others.

Hank's practice is multidimensional. He has to get out of his normal operating strategies, which include the automatic generation of thoughts and feelings. He has to look around and see how his environment is currently affecting him. He has to think – I mean really think, about what there is to learn right now beyond perceived constraints. He has to accept that what he thought would be the rewards and outcome of this position isn't forthcoming. Yet, there are greater rewards far more rich, delicious and sustainable for him to achieve, right here, right now. Hank can get – and is getting, that this is a leadership development opportunity of a lifetime. It isn't available in any MBA program; not even at Harvard Business School. If he can shift his attitude and perspective, Hank will become an exceptional leader and manager.

We all have dreams about what we imagine our careers will reap. More often than not, we see it happening faster and better than it actually occurs. We get frustrated, pissed off and resentful when it doesn't look the way we imagined. As we take each step into being an adult, realizing that life doesn't always show up the way we want, we have a much greater capacity to choose willingly to explore the opportunities for growth and learning that are right in front of us. By meeting what feels like demands with openness and curiosity, we will be given the rewards we anticipated in ways we've yet to imagine.

Though it appears as if Hank's manager is inept at his job, he will actually be one of the greatest contributors to Hank's development as an up-and-coming leader. However, it's up to Hank to fully utilize his time under his guidance to benefit from his mentor's style.

19: Exchanging self-importance for Self-Importance

During our first corporate coaching session, Brandy, a manager at a furniture manufacturing company, shared that over the years she's found herself experiencing the same frustration over and over again. Regardless of the company she works for – and there have been several over the past seven years, she keeps anticipating that any day now, people will see her value and importance and she'll be given the accolades and promotion she's entitled too. "I was in the top ten of my class in my MBA program; I always work more hours and contribute more than any other person in my department; I've been here the longest and I'm the easiest person to get along with."

Brandy's list of I, I, I's, goes on and on, and yet, time and time again, she gets passed over. Does this make sense to you? Doesn't it make you wonder why a person with such an outstanding self-report isn't getting the expected promotions?

What is it about the Brandy's-of-the-world, who are so valuable, and at the same time aren't promoted based on their own perceived merits? If not Brandy, then who and why?

The truth is, nobody cares how smart Brandy is, how many hours she works or her degrees. Her very demeanor discounts, dismisses and devalues other people. She doesn't have to say or do anything. Nobody likes being shamed, guilted or blamed for being less than by someone who emanates entitled, righteous arrogance.

It's confusing for the Brandy's-of-the-world. They think to themselves: "Other people must see how special, unique and important I am. There must be something wrong with them." So, the Brandy's-of-the world go looking for another company to work for with people who will see their value and worth.

Interestingly enough, all of us have some degree of Brandy within us. We all have a sense of self-importance and entitlement. Brandy's self-importance quite often is annoying to most of us because it's a reflection of that aspect in ourselves that wants or needs to be acknowledged and admired for the gifts we bring to the world. When we are overlooked or passed over, indignation and resentment arise, and our need to be seen triggers outbursts. We, like Brandy, become impossible to be around. I hate to think I'm like Brandy!

This is a tricky subject but one that needs attention. We have to deal with the Brandy's-of-the- world and we also have to deal with the internal Brandy, who relentlessly has us feel resentful and angry when we aren't being treated with the degree of respect we think we deserve. How do we figure out what's true about our self-importance – what's really real?

People like, respect and promote individuals who use their gifts in collaboration with others; who don't try to better themselves at the expense of their co-workers or the company at large. We all know what this feels like. Insidious and subtle; too often we don't even know when it's being done to us and we don't even know we are doing it to others or ourselves.

I admit to being one of these individuals who believed that because I have three Masters Degrees and a Ph.D. that I was special and should be treated as such. And, after writing my first book, *Self-Empowerment 101*, I really thought I should become world-renowned. It didn't happen – at least not in the way I envisioned. I thought: "What's the point of doing all of this work if no one is going to see how important I am?"

My self-importance shattered in three different arenas of my life, simultaneously (Career, family and marriage). OW!! Within each of these areas I truly believed I was entitled to a prestigious position.

I believe most mid-life crises are founded on this one critical and devastating blow to our egoic identity, leaving us with a disintegration of who we think we are. It isn't fun – trust me; however, the process reveals that we are so much more important and our contributions are far more valuable than our ego-self allows us to believe.

Through this process, I became conscious that, to a large degree, my self-importance served my sense of entitlement, arrogance and righteousness. True Self-Importance serves my Highest Truth, our Highest Good and my Highest Contributions to the World.

A specific intention I serve in my coaching practice is to empower my clients to minimize the impact of the mid-life crisis – the shattering that must occur in order to realize and actualize the Self that we've all come here to know. Through conversations, I encourage clients to shift their interpretations and to think beyond their own personal and limited perspective.

Each of us can dismantle our ego – our personal identity, by paying attention to signs along the way. These signs are everywhere and always guiding us. When we don't pay attention, we'll initially experience a slight nagging feeling or irritation. If we ignore these, we will feel a nudge and then a shove. And, if we still persist in ignoring the signs, we will experience an "out of this world" disruption, which will have us be exclaiming, "Man, I never saw that coming!"

Brandy is waking up to the fact that her achievements don't make her truly effective at bringing her fullest contribution to her personal and professional life. She is digging deeper to discover a more expanded bounty of gifts that are hers and hers only to share. It will mean a re-orienting of her reality. By cultivating such awareness she will minimize her shattering; at the same time expand beyond belief, her true Self-Importance.

20: Dilemmas Just Keep on Coming

A couple of months ago, a colleague of mine commented on one of my blogs. They pointed out that perhaps I was out of integrity with regard to some of the content I was sharing. Though I determined that I had not been out of integrity in any way, the fact that I had been called on it really shook me – enough to shut down my practice of writing until now.

Writing is just one of my businesses, along with coaching and teaching. Like any businessperson, a very human response can be triggered by a professional suggestion or comment. What got triggered for me was a core "truth" I've lived with for as long as I can remember, that sooner or later would be revealed. That "truth" was that I was a fraud – an unethical fraud at that! I work very hard to be in integrity, as I have the utmost respect for people's privacy and what is shared in conversations, sessions, courses and workshops. So, my colleague's comment shook me to the bone.

Most of my writing comes from an idea or insight, or from a comment that was made, or a story shared, which, from my perspective, is universal and relevant to countless human beings. I love writing about these facets of humanity, exploring the deep, raw nature of who we are inside our human dilemmas. This time the dilemma is mine.

My spontaneous and fairly effortless writing stopped as I questioned the purpose of writing at all. "Who cares about what I write?" – was the first rhetorical question that arose. The second was "What's the point?" The third was: "What difference does it make if or what I write?"

There's something under all of these questions that had avoided discovery. As long as I ignored any urge to write, I figured I could avoid that – whatever it is. However, in service to my commitment to finishing this series and to my craft, I must write. And, in service to my own integrity I willingly engage in an expedition in search of that which remains concealed, and share with you my own professional dilemmas.

The dilemma is that, on one hand, what may be revealed could be nasty, stinky and messy – aspects of myself that I never want to know about, let alone reveal to others. On the other hand, I consider myself to be an artist, and by continuing to avoid this expedition, well, I might as well take up golf, because as long as I hide from the truth, my writing will have no point.

"The truth shall set you free." We've all heard this statement, but to really connect to that truth is far scarier than the words alone suggest.

In this moment, I'm avoiding vulnerability, scorn and condescension; deep humiliation and annihilation of my self. I know the experience of annihilation perhaps from childhood or teenage years when my egoic self was so fragile and I was shattered by someone's disparaging words. I've done my best to avoid any possible repeat of this experience. Through decades of successes, you'd think that I'd have moved past such strong reactions to one single comment. Nope. We are never done because we never stop being human.

I have no doubt that the majority of us humans live with the fact that we are inadequate to face every circumstance with perfection. We live with self-contempt because of our mistakes, often resulting in agonizing guilt and shame. It is so painful to realize that we really are powerless in the face of being imperfect in an imperfect world. There's no doubt: it can be excruciating!

That's what makes it all so perfect, though. In all of this there is a HUGE lesson that can only be learned when facing our deepest and worst fears: that we are the only people on the face of the planet that struggle with such inadequacy. We also sit with the fear of what will happen when the inevitable moment occurs: when we are found out.

How most of us face these fears and truths is by doing what I did: ignore and avoid, distract and deny, and pretend I didn't really want to write. We focus on something else – something we do well, where we are less vulnerable to attack. Although this keeps me safe, it doesn't allow me to bring my highest and best contributions to the world. It doesn't allow the fullest expression of my essential self! In such a dilemma, I have to choose. And, whatever I choose will set me in the direction fraught with risk of vulnerability – no escaping that!

Over the years, I've grown my ability to write about the layers of human experience underlying our daily lives. I'm committed to push through my own invulnerability in order to meet that place in myself that feels so fragile. I do this because I know myself to be a normal human being, and by exploring and uncovering my own existential dilemmas, perhaps I can encourage others to feel safe in exploring their own human self – beyond who they think themselves to be. It really isn't so bad once you begin the journey, especially if you have a coach or companion to support you through the process.

Our work in the world provides us with an exquisite arena within which to gently touch the edges of our comfort zone. We can do this in service to expanding our contribution to fellow office mates, teams, organizations, families, communities, and to the world. And, although all the recipients of our gifts are important, unless we experience the fulfillment at our soul level, we will not experience the outcome we anticipated. We have to want it enough to step out beyond the precipice. We have to want it enough to step out beyond what we know – out into the mystery. YIKES!

As many of us know, and you've heard me say this before: we all are required to engage in the expedition of a lifetime. You get to choose in what manner you wish to begin. My choice is to willingly go, thus minimizing the struggle and maximizing the Wha-Hoo!

21: 80% Effective

Michael, a COO of a growing startup in Austin, Texas, is a great guy and a brilliant thinker. He's been hired by a particular company to bring about a turnaround in management and inevitably the bottom line. The company has experienced a significant loss in revenue over the past few months and it's now Michael's job to turn things around. If he fails, the company will fold – end of story.

Michael is about to take the company in a direction that will transform its vision, culture and business structure. There's no doubt he has what it takes to create this turnaround. However, he's challenged and stopped with every step he takes. For instance, yesterday he received a memo from his CEO that states all unnecessary expenditures will be cut. There goes any actualization of executive team off-sites to thoroughly discuss and implement what's required to make this company work.

Michael is stymied and feels like his hands are tied! He is out to rescue the company. That's what he's been hired to do. Since joining four months ago, he's been exploring the underlying foundation upon which to rebuild. He doesn't want to push too hard for change as the company and executive team is also quite new and pretty fragile. He fears resistance and pushback. Michael retreats from potential conflict or confrontation; unsure whether the executive team will follow his lead. Our coaching conversations lean into what might occur if he steps into his role to a larger degree.

I asked Michael to assess the degree of effectiveness that he brings with him to his job. He answers that he's about 80% effective. For Michael's personal and professional development and for the sake of the company, he's going to have to stretch to 82-85% to fully engage the company in this campaign.

You expected me to say that Michael needs to stretch to 100%, didn't you? Well, given that for Michael, 80% is within his comfort zone, to leap too far beyond the edge could create a backlash. And, as most of us have experienced, if we push ourselves too hard for change, we end up digging in our own heels, resisting and pushing back. Exploring out just a couple of degrees from the edge of Michael's comfort zone allows him to experience various dimensions of reality that confront him, without leaving the comfort of his easy chair. From here, he can assess and evaluate any number of strategies that would initiate a greater degree of effectiveness. Though he initially leans out just a bit, he actually expands his comfort zone, engaging his fullest potential to explore and experiment with his capacity to make things happen.

It's actually rare for leaders to operate at 100% effectiveness. And, my belief is that most companies aren't even going to hire an individual who brings that degree of effectiveness to the workplace, because they are yet to be capable of that level of success themselves. They don't yet know how to bring about that level of success. That makes sense!

Quite a few executive clients of mine back away from the edge of their comfort zone because it's unfamiliar territory. They fear what may be revealed. More to the point, they fear experiencing the inadequacy within their humanity, which no doubt will devastate their egoic identity. Who are they without the suit of armor called ME?

The consequence of avoiding the edge may mean that employees and the company at large are unlikely to fulfill their vision. Executives are human beings, and like most of us, they may miss the point of digging through personal baggage and exposing vulnerabilities, along with the nuggets of GOLD! They play a big game, however, more often than not, they are unwilling to risk their own personal security in order to remain invulnerable.

Much of Michael's conversation with me thus far has been how the company is resisting, ignoring or limiting his authority. As his thinking partner, my listening informs me that, on some unconscious level, the company is conspiring to bring Michael to the fullest expression of his essential nature and for him to lead from this place. They won't budge until he brings more of his empowered self to the table. He is required to empower himself to make those shifts in order to empower others to do the same.

As Michael and I talk, he begins to get the lay of the land within himself and his company. He's beginning to see how, in many ways, the company is waiting for him to step into the very practice he's going to require of them. He sees now that he has to be the role model for change.

Regardless of how high up in the ranks of leadership one climbs, each individual is required to face their fears and risk vulnerability, only in service to their vision and life purpose. I love working with Michael because he is clearly aware of a larger vision for his company and he has a knowing that this is essential for the company to thrive, or even to survive.

The Dilemma for Michael: he can stay within his 80% effectiveness and capitulate to the company's foot-dragging, while still maintaining his reputation as an effective leader. Or, he can amp up a few degrees of effectiveness, risking a loss of safety and security. He may be vulnerable to the possibility that people won't like him, may confront him and perhaps drastically push back. Yet change is required to save the company. He's considering his options.

Michael didn't get to be a COO by being a coward. He's talented, highly effective and has what it takes to create this turnaround. He has no idea yet the fullest potential available to him just beyond that 80%. I'm happy to report that he sees this as an exciting adventure! Wha-hoo!

Summing it Up

As you've read each story, I suspect you were hoping to find resolution – a happy ending for each businessman and woman. I used to look forward to writing those happy endings myself. However, over time, what has been revealed is that the resolution of one dilemma engages the beginning of the next. Inhale. Exhale. Now, a new dilemma begins. Themes may repeat with subtle nuances, but the next learning opportunity will show up on cue, even though you never made the request.

Unraveling and untangling the dynamics of a dilemma can take hours, days, weeks or longer, depending on the degree of attachment one has to beliefs and the limited outcomes derived from them. Interpretations, thought processes and strategies have been carefully cultivated over lifetimes to bring each person to this choice-point in their personal and professional career.

By now, you may realize that a dilemma is like a multi-dimensional being with a life of its own. It thrives on complexity and emotional angst. It doesn't want you to actually choose, then follow through with action, because then that dilemma would cease to be, and a new dilemma will replace it.

Thriving (Not Surviving) in Business

With things changing in every corner of the planet and in just about every aspect of life, our relationship to security, stability, and surviving are rapidly changing.

Over decades we've built the ground of our being on industrial, corporate and professional success. Many of us have attempted to define our fulfillment by our place within the corporate structure. That is all changing as we come to realize that climbing the corporate ladder just ain't what it's cracked up to be. It never has been.

Letting go of the American Dream, one that has now been embraced across the globe, at first seems to be death itself. "I've lost my soul," is a statement I hear from corporate clients, from the top of the ladder and all the way down. The fact of the matter is that too many of us – something like four out of five people-- are actually suffering, settling and merely *surviving* within their current work environment. That means only one in five people actually experience job satisfaction. Perhaps letting go of this American Dream is actually what is in order.

What is required in order to thrive in the business world is letting go of *any*thing and *every*thing that has you suffer, settle and survive. This includes any and all interpretations you carry that have you live, work and be far, far away from your highest truth and your greatest contribution to the world.

Rudyard Kipling's poem: *If*, sums up for me what's required to thrive within our business environment.

"If you can keep your head when all about you are losing theirs and blaming it on you;

If you can trust yourself when all men doubt you, make allowance for their doubting too:

If you can wait and not be tired by waiting, or, being lied about, don't deal in lies, or being hated don't give way to hating, and yet don't look too good, nor talk too wise;

If you can dream and not make dreams your master; If you can think and not make thoughts your aim; If you can meet with Triumph and Disaster, and treat those two impostors just the same:

If you can bear to hear the truth you've spoken twisted by knaves to make a trap for fools, or watch the things you gave your life to, broken, and stoop and build'em up with worn-out tools;

If you can make one heap of all your winnings and risk it on one turn of pitch-and-toss, and lose, and start again at your beginnings, and never breathe a word about your loss:

If you can force your heart and nerve and sinew to serve your turn long after they are gone, and so hold on when there is nothing in you except the Will which says to them: "Hold on!"

If you can talk with crowds and keep your virtue, or walk with Kings nor lose the common touch, if neither foes nor loving friends can hurt you, if all men count with you, but none too much: If you can fill the unforgiving minute with sixty seconds' worth of distance run, yours is the Earth and everything that's in it, and, which is more, you'll be a Man, my son!"

To thrive in an environment that relentlessly foists mayhem at your feet and constantly demands presence and awareness to how you, and only you, choose to choose to make your highest and best contribution to the world, remember:

1. Keep your head when all about you are losing theirs:" Succumbing to fear, deception and lies will continually lead you towards the certain death of your soul and spirit – the core of your being. Discern *your* truth and be willing to take actions from this truth, *not* from what others tell you is true.

2. Trust yourself – hold the vision for a quality of being that fulfills and nourishes your soul.

3. Honor yourself, your own thoughts, your own feelings, and your own needs and wants.

4. Notice whether you are being and acting in alignment with your vision, and your spirit. You can remain in your current position and be aligned with your vision and your integrity.

5. Each corporate body, including governments and religious institutions, is inherently good, not evil. The vision and mission of each of these entities however, has too often been lost or forgotten by those who lead in order to gain power. The fact is that all of us, regardless of who we lead, do so based on personal beliefs and interpretations, most of which are rooted, not in what we've learned regarding right practices, but in our own personal, fear-based belief system. Fear-based leadership inevitably corrupts the environment, and as a consequence, loftier visions and dedication to the mission disappear. To thrive in this world, every

organization will have to *return* to its Core Vision of purpose that inspired its inception.

6. Consider that from a more Universal perspective, disasters are no worse or better than triumphs. They both require humility, respect and a deep presence to what is. Both require engagement with the deepest and most profound level of who you are inside the experience. You may receive promotions, bonuses and accolades, you may receive a boot out the door; either way the experience will bring you to your most essential self – one that is raw, human and so alive!

7. Bear witness to the eventuality that the very things you've given your life to will become broken and unmendable. This will be one of many rites of passage. Facing the worst disasters cleanses us of attachments to those interpretations of what we believe to be of value, what we believe to be true; and leaves us purged and clear-sighted. Many people have realized the gift in having been shaken loose from their clutches of suffering, settling and surviving. Their life has become simple, more in alignment with their highest truth and with their life purpose. They've found more fulfillment with less stuff.

8. Be mindful and compassionate of everyone who touches your life. They are no different from you, in that they too are in the midst of dilemmas that shake their reality and their sense of self. They too face moments that threaten their perspective, facing potential humiliation and ruin. They too are attempting to balance integrity with job security. They, like you,

question what's required to survive. However, how many of us question what's required to thrive?

The business environment is an incredibly rich world within which to cultivate such a practice as what Mr. Kipling suggests. It requires one to exercise muscles of conscious choice-making in service to essential truth and knowing of what this is *all* about. Moreover, the demands and stress of the work, the relationships, even the sometimes toxic physical environment, all require, perhaps, just simple remembering that really and truly, we are all doing our best.

As I've expressed in the introduction to this book, extraordinary people challenge themselves to detach from dilemmas in service to something greater than their egoic selves. They willingly embark on expeditions that cultivate more expanded intelligence in themselves and the people with whom they work. Adventuring past their comfort zone, they reveal truths they knew existed, but they never fathomed what it would take to engage with them.

Threads of each dilemma are woven deeply in our childhood relationships. The corporate environment more often than not, reflects our family systems and cultures. These systems are filled with opportunities to engage the strategies we cultivated as children. Using what wisdom and maturity we had, we made sense of the world and, in most cases, continue to utilize the same choice-making processes and strategies. We learn through these current opportunities to deal with environments that challenged us as children. History, as you know, will repeat itself until the required lessons are learned.

Through coaching sessions, clients consciously cultivate and strengthen their capacity to choose to thrive by seeing the world differently. They choose to practice alternative strategies, which inevitably bring about the outcome they've envisioned. They have a knowing of what's true, and at the same time they have to practice faith. They have to risk vulnerability, and face seemingly undesirable consequences. Potential rejection, humiliation and annihilation of everything they've come to believe about themselves and reality at large, could ensue. Underlying values will be discovered and distinguished, which will shift the course of the dilemma one way or another. Making choices brings a person face to face with vulnerability, while at the same time gaining momentum toward their desired trajectory.

Michael – in the previous chapter, came into our session today sharing an extraordinary unfolding. He realized that the potential for transformation within the culture of his company could only occur through his own willingness to expand his personal repertoire of choice-making strategies, in relation to the dilemmas that face him at every turn. "It's not about the employees or the executive team – it's all about me!" He got it! And he got that there is a great deal of work ahead of him in service to attaining the highest degree of integrity and commitment required in order to make his best contribution to the planet.

Dilemmas are choice-points. Seeing that every choice-point is an opportunity to either choose to move along the trajectory of one's vision, or to follow the well-worn path of least resistance, this is where extraordinary people recreate themselves. Exercising muscles of discernment, utilizing untapped intelligence

– cognitive, emotional, somatic and spiritual: it's all required in order to find the clarity to resolve underlying conflicts that keep most of us stuck.

Understanding how one engages in the process of choice-making won't make dilemmas disappear. They will never, ever disappear. But as we begin to "unpack" our choice-making process, we become more effective in understanding the dynamics of each dilemma, and the values and hierarchy of commitments we have in place that actually create the dilemma in the first place.

The personal element will always compound any dilemma. Inquiry into the hierarchy of commitments reveals which intention, value or commitment is getting attention over others. It's an opportunity to ask – "Is this really what I'm committed to?"

The unfolding of our lives and how we 'be' in life will always be perfectly imperfect. This is so we have a multitude of opportunities to discover and declare our truths and the values, and the intentions and commitments that serve those truths when faced with the edge of our comfort zone once immersed in a new dilemma. Generating strength, wisdom, faith, intelligence and curiosity will bring you onto your path and only your path. Hopefully, you will continually be amazed and delighted to discover more of who you are with every dilemma you explore.

Remembering to be your truest self, as best you can, may save you in the midst of a dilemma, for it is an incredible act of courage to release yourself from self-judgment. This sole act will bring about the capacity to repeat this process over and over; the outcome being a sense of thriving as the fullest expression of your essential self.

Acknowledgments

Kim Harris is a great editor. Sincerity and commitment to perfection are two of the many qualities that have made working with her fun and rewarding.

Himanshu Jhamb and ActiveGarage.com have inspired me to write what I write. I so appreciate his believing in me and his earnest desire to provide great content for his readers.

Maureen O'Neill is a fabulous graphic artist. She pops with ideas and is amazingly tuned-in to her clients' way of being. She is delightful and engaging to work with.

I am so inspired by my clients. Our sessions together reveal patterns and processes that are universal in nature. As they cultivate awareness and shift how they are being, they generate the outcomes they desire. They validate this way of thinking about business by the very results they create for themselves. And the effects of their shifts ripple out to the Universe

Bio

Rosie is considered to be a preeminent thought leader in the field of Transformational Coaching, Transformational Coach Training and Transformational Leadership Facilitation. She is the author of the popular books '*Self-Empowerment 101,*' and recently published '*the ABC's of Spirituality in Business.*' Founder of The Paradigm Shifts Coaching Group, she specializes in empowering individuals, executives and organizations to fearlessly embrace transformation and to realize untapped potential.

Rosie resides on Orcas Island, WA